The Beach Lover's Guide to the Outer Banks

Volume 1: Kitty Hawk, Kill Devil Hills, and Nags Head

The Beach Lover's Guide to the Outer Banks

Volume 1: Kitty Hawk, Kill Devil Hills, and Nags Head

The Beach Road and Beyond

By Tamara Hoffmann Shipp

Copyright © 2020 Tamara Hoffmann Shipp
All rights reserved.

Cover Design by Sarah Glaser

ISBN: 9781656576781

Dedicated to My Grandmother

Jacqueline Fleming Hoffmann
(1911-1995)

Grandmommy loved the beach. When we went on vacation together, she had a different bathing suit for each day. If she ever put her toe in the water, I never saw it, but she loved to people-watch and bask in the soothing sound of the ocean.

This one's for you, Grandmommy.

Table of Contents

Introduction i
Chapter 1 - A Brief History of the Outer Banks 1
Chapter 2 - The Beach Road 7
Chapter 3 - Vacation Rentals 24
Chapter 4 - The Beaches 48
Chapter 5 - Totally OBX Things to Do 67
Chapter 6 - Budget-friendly activities 84
Chapter 7 - Water Activities 99
Chapter 8 - Kid Friendly Activities 106
Chapter 9 - Rainy Day Activities 112
Chapter 10 - But Wait! There's More! 117
Chapter 11 - Restaurants 121
Chapter 12 - Shopping 140
Chapter 13 - Off-Season Activities 144
Chapter 14 - Conserving the Beauty 149
Chapter 15 - Can't Get Enough? 152
Chapter 16 - Important Resources 155

Introduction

My relationship with the Outer Banks of North Carolina began in the late 1970s. My parents had taken up camping a few years earlier and, in their search for a place to pitch their tent, had discovered the Outer Banks. I did not tag along on the camping trips. I did not then — nor do I now — "do" camping. My idea of roughing it is a night at a chain motel. But when my folks ditched the tent and started renting a beach house, I decided to give the Outer Banks a try.

And I fell in love.

> *Everything about it and the fierce old coast around it had the ring and taste and feel of utter rightness to me. Its peace and loneliness crept into my veins and ran there, its wildness called out to the deep buried wildness in my heart.*
> — *Anne Rivers Siddons, Outer Banks*

My mother referred to the area south of Oregon Inlet as the "real Outer Banks," in contrast to the Kitty Hawk/Kill Devil Hills/Nags Head area, which my folks considered more touristy. My next book will focus on that area, from Rodanthe south to Hatteras, as well as Ocracoke, but for this volume, most of my discussion and recommendations will be limited to the more developed parts of the Outer Banks, from Kitty Hawk to Nags Head, as well as Manteo.

(For those interested in the Northern Beaches, from Southern Shores to Corolla, volume three of this series will cover those areas.)

My parents preferred to stay in Avon, which is about 45 miles south of Nags Head. Sometimes we would spend two weeks there, where the only activity was … the beach.

In those days, the only "grocery store" in Avon was a small mom-and-pop gas station with a convenience store that offered a limited food selection. I believe it was called the Avon shopping center, though "shopping" was definitely a bit of a stretch. You could pick up a loaf of bread and a jar of peanut butter but not much more. Also, Avon, at that time, was a dry town. So we had to bring with us not only all the groceries we needed for two weeks but also any "adult beverages" we wanted while on vacation, and then all of it had to be hauled up one or two sets of stairs, since all the houses are set on pilings, and many of them have what's known as a "reverse floor plan" where the kitchen and living room are on the top floor, with the bedrooms on the first floor.

Cable TV was many years from reaching that part of the Outer Banks — hence, most rental houses didn't even have TVs. Radio was spotty, so we had to settle for whatever station we could pick up. We had no cell phones, no laptops, and no DVD players. As a result, we read a lot of books. Most beach rental houses — even now — have take-one/leave-one libraries. Selections can range from steamy romance novels to classics. On one vacation, I recall reading H.G. Wells' *First Men in the Moon*. I also read *From Here to Eternity*.

But if you love the beach, as I do, there was no better place in the world to take a vacation. In fact, when my husband and I were married in 1984, we agreed that Avon was the perfect place for a honeymoon. We had no need for tourist attractions or fancy restaurants. As newlyweds, all we wanted was to be together ... alone. No better place for that than the Outer Banks.

We certainly got what we wished for. It was the third week of September — kids back in school, tourists back home dreaming of next year's vacation — and there we were, just the two of us, in a round house, oceanfront, on the edge of the Cape Hatteras National Seashore.

One somewhat surprising feature in the tiny town of Avon was that it had a movie theater. *Ghostbusters* had been released that summer, and it was playing at the Avon Cinema. One evening we decided to have a dinner-and-a-movie night. We ate at a casual little restaurant called the Froggy Dog — at the time of publication, it was still there — then headed to the movie theater, anxious to see the blockbuster people had been raving about. When we walked up to the ticket booth, we were told we were the only ones who had showed up so far and that they could not run the movie unless at least eight customers were in the theater. They invited us to wait to see if anyone else arrived. We waited. No one else showed up. No movie for us that night.

Fast forward 10 years or so to the early 1990s. My husband and I had relocated from northern Virginia to the Hampton Roads area in southeastern Virginia. As a result, our travel time to the Outer Banks was reduced from about six hours to just a little over one hour. We had two little boys by then, and it was a few years before we got back to taking vacations, but when we did, we decided that the "touristy" part of the Outer Banks was more suited to the needs of our boys and their friends.

So, we started renting an oceanfront cottage every summer in Kill Devil Hills. For several years in a row, we rented the same house for the 4th of July, in a location within stumbling distance of Awful Arthur's Oyster Bar and the Avalon Fishing Pier. The house was a classic beach cottage, like something straight out of the movie *Summer of '42*. It had been rescued from the sea at one point and moved 100 yards west to keep it from being claimed by the ocean. Some of the original pilings were still there. A couple of them had been repurposed to build a bench. The house had no air conditioning. None. Not even window units. But it had lots of windows and was right on the ocean. The master bedroom had its own oceanfront balcony, so we slept at night with the sliding doors open, falling asleep to the soothing sound of the Atlantic.

For the last 20 years, with few exceptions, the Outer Banks has been our go-to vacation destination. Because we live within about an hour's drive of Kitty Hawk, we frequently take day trips to get our beach fix and soak in the negative ions. At one point, we even owned a second home in Kill Devil Hills.

Insider Tip: Negative ions are molecules present in the air in certain locations. The beach is one of those locations. Released by the pounding of the waves on the sand, we breathe in these negative ions. Once they enter the bloodstream, they cause an increase in serotonin levels. Serotonin is believed to reduce stress and depression, as well as boost energy levels. There is solid science to back up these claims, and it accounts for why being at the beach produces wonderful feelings of well-being and relaxation. (It also accounts for why we often have some of our most inspired breakthrough thoughts when we're in the shower, since negative ions are also released when water hits the tub or shower stall.)

The Outer Banks is truly my favorite place in the world.

About this book

First, let me tell you what this is book is *not*. It's not a guide to help you find the best price on a hotel. In general, you won't find ticket prices and hours of operation for attractions, although in some cases such information is included for the sake of completeness.

This book is a genuine insider's guide to the Outer Banks — not a cookie-cutter travel book produced by a company that churns out vacation guides by the dozen for hundreds of different locations. It is written by someone who truly loves the Outer Banks and has spent countless weeks enjoying its serene beauty, as well as the craziness brought on by the summer crowds. Keep in mind that, for the most part, this book is limited to the Kitty Hawk/Kill Devil Hills/Nags Head area. I do include some information on Manteo, home of The Lost Colony, as well as the Northern Beaches (after all, that's where the wild horses are). I touch briefly on areas as far south as Ocracoke Island, since many vacationers want to see the Cape Hatteras lighthouse and take a ride on the Ocracoke Island ferry. Volume two of this book series will focus more in-depth on areas south of Oregon Inlet, followed by volume three, focusing on the Northern Beaches of the Outer Banks.

This book won't provide you with the price points and star ratings for every restaurant, but I *will* tell you about some of my favorite places and provide some **Insider Tips** (in bold throughout this book) — everything from what to order to where to sit. In Chapter 2, as we take a "virtual" ride down the Beach Road, I point out the hotels and restaurants along Route 12 and include brief descriptions. For a complete listing of hotels, check Chapter 3, and to find a town-by-town listing of restaurants, along with a description of their menu, go to Chapter 5.

I've included listings and descriptions of the most popular attractions, and I'll give you plenty of ideas for activities, including those you can do for free (or almost free), as well as rainy day activities and how you can find bargains on beach supplies and souvenirs. You'll find information on just about every water activity you can think of — what they are, where to take lessons, and where to rent equipment or take a guided tour. I've also included information on fishing and golf. And while I still don't "do" camping, I know many people love it, so you'll find a list of campgrounds to help you find the perfect spot to pitch your tent or park your RV.

Insider Tip: The crowds can get pretty heavy in the summer. Restaurants often have long waits, grocery stores are packed, and traffic can be a bear. Don't let it ruin your vacation. It's all about attitude. Learn to view the noisy children on the beach with appreciation, rather than annoyance. Let them remind you of your own childhood, either the one you had or the one you wish you'd had. If you find yourself standing in a long line at the grocery store, strike up a conversation with those around you. It can be fun to find out where people are from. Since restaurants are typically very busy in the summer, consider doing brunch instead of breakfast or plan a late dinner. In other words, go with the flow. If you're like a lot of people, this may be your one week of vacation for the year. Decide ahead of time that nothing will deter you from enjoying it and being happy. (If all else fails, walk down to the beach and soak up some of those negative ions.)

In this book, you will find a practical guide to planning your Outer Banks vacation, from packing to traveling. I'll give you ideas for what to what to do if you arrive early and you need to keep the kids occupied while waiting to get the key to your rental house. I'll tell you where you can shop for groceries, where to find the best seafood (from fresh markets to full-service restaurants), and when is the best time of year to bargain shop. You'll learn which beaches get crowded in the summer and where to find beaches that are off the beaten path, as well as safety rules and precautions, and how you can help preserve the beauty of the Outer Banks. I've included listings of the best attractions, as well as some ideas for rainy day activities. In addition, there's information about off-season activities and annual festivals. I'll introduce you to some of the wildlife you may see in the Outer Banks, as well as rules about interacting with the wild horses and loggerhead turtles. (Spoiler alert: *Don't*.) You'll also find lots of links to make it easy for you to get more information on the activities and attractions that interest you, as well as emergency numbers, medical clinics, and other services you may need during your stay.

In recent years, I've spent most of my time on the Outer Banks in the Kitty Hawk to Nags Head area, which is why this book focuses mostly on those towns, as well as Manteo. I do touch on other areas, however, because even if you stay in, say, Kill Devil Hills, you very well may want to take an excursion to the north or south to discover some of the other uniquely Outer Banks sites to see. For a more in-depth look at points south of Oregon Inlet, keep an eye out for volume two of this series.

One last note about this book: With the exception of a few Amazon affiliate links, no compensation of any kind has been solicited or accepted from any of the businesses listed. The descriptions and opinions are my own, with absolutely no direct input from the management of any of the businesses included herein.

What makes the Outer Banks different?

Back in the 1970s, when I first started going to the Outer Banks, the area was still a well-kept secret. But thanks to regional publicity efforts and road improvements, it has become a very popular vacation destination — with good reason.

As I write this book, I am located in my home office, which is about a 30-minute drive from the oceanfront at

Virginia Beach. Yet, when we want to relax and enjoy an afternoon by the water's edge, we never go to Virginia Beach. We only go to what we call "the oceanfront" (as opposed to "the beach") when we want to bar-hop or attend an event, such as a concert or the boardwalk art show or have a look at the magnificent sand sculptures that are part of the Neptune Festival every September.

The Outer Banks is where we go to "the beach." To be sure, there has been a lot of development in the Outer Banks since my first visit back in the '70s, but the individual beach cottages still far outnumber the hotels, and there are very few "high-rise" hotels between Kitty Hawk and Nags Head. (Most have fewer than 5 floors.) There is no boardwalk. Much of the Outer Banks is protected park land where loggerhead sea turtles' nest and development are not allowed.

Whether we visit for a day, a weekend, or a week, our go-to spot is usually the Cape Hatteras National Seashore, Ramp 4, across from the Oregon Inlet Marina. In years past, this area was more accessible, but protected species such as nesting seabirds and loggerhead turtles required officials to cordon off certain parts of what locals call The Point. In addition, driving on the beach now requires a permit. While some visitors are disappointed that access is no longer free, it's actually been beneficial, in my opinion. By requiring a permit, the National Park Service has been able to cut down on the number of people who go out to the beach in their four-wheel-drive vehicles and "behave badly," driving too fast and taking too many chances. Nowadays, most of the people on the beach at Ramp 4 are looking for a relaxing day on the beach, whether that means fishing, playing cornhole, or just settling in with a good book.

So, let's get started. I'll begin with a bit of history, and then we'll take a drive down the Beach Road.

Chapter 1 - A Brief History of the Outer Banks

It's hard to know where to begin with the telling of Outer Banks history. These barrier islands have been a witness to events that have shaped not only the story of our country but the trajectory of mankind. Native Americans inhabited the islands long before the early English settlers arrived in the New World. Several Outer Banks towns have Native American names, such as Manteo, Kinnakeet, Ocracoke, and Hatteras, a tribute to the original inhabitants of the area.

For the most part, Native Americans welcomed the early settlers who arrived in the 16th century. Unfortunately, the settlers brought with them diseases to which Native Americans had not previously been exposed. As a result, large numbers of natives died, and within 100 years, most tribes had disappeared from the Outer Banks.

In this chapter, I'll review just a few of the remarkable events that have helped to build the culture and folklore of the Outer Banks.

Firstborn — and an Enduring Mystery

It's likely you remember learning in school about The Lost Colony and the one clue they left behind — the word "Croatoan" scrawled on a tree. Well, the Outer Banks is where that happened.

The first English child born in the New World was Virginia Dare, born on August 18, 1657, at Fort Raleigh on Roanoke Island, which is situated between Croatan Sound and Roanoke Sound. The colonists had been sent by Sir Walter Raleigh to establish the first English colony and permanent settlement in the New World, with John White leading the team and acting as mayor of the colony. White's daughter, Eleanor Dare, gave birth shortly after their arrival. When White returned from a trip to England, having traveled back to gather more supplies, he discovered all the colonists, including his own family, had vanished. Archaeological digs have turned up some hopeful clues, but the circumstances of their disappearance continue to puzzle historians to this day.

Insider Tip: "America's Greatest Unsolved Mystery" is brought to life in an outdoor production at Fort Raleigh National Historical Site in Manteo. *The Lost Colony*, the play, was first staged in 1937. Intended to run only for that one summer, it attracted the attention of President Franklin D. Roosevelt, who attended the show in August of 1937, sparking interest that has kept the play in production ever since. Today it remains one of the most popular attractions on the Outer Banks, with shows every summer from June through the end of August. The most famous alumnus of *The Lost Colony* is Andy Griffith, who began performing in the play in the 1940s. Griffith made his home in Manteo for many years, until his death in 2012. For more information on the play and to purchase tickets in advance, visit The Lost Colony website.

There be pirates here!

Legendary pirate Blackbeard, whose real name was Edward Teach, chose Pamlico Sound as one of his favorite plundering grounds and was a frequent visitor in Ocracoke Island, where an inlet, Teach's Hole, was named for him. Teach's pirate ship, a captured French merchant vessel, was named *Queen Anne's Revenge* and equipped with 40 guns. Nicknamed Blackbeard because of his thick facial hair, he was said to have a fearsome appearance and would tie lit twine under his hat to scare his enemies. He relied on his frightening image to intimidate those he robbed, but despite the modern image of bloodthirsty pirates, Blackbeard was not known to physically harm or murder his victims. In the early 18th century, residents of North Carolina, tired of Blackbeard's ways, enlisted the help of Virginia Governor Alexander Spotswood, who commissioned a crew of navy officers to track him down. On November 22, 1718, Blackbeard was killed by Lt. Robert Maynard of the Royal Navy in Ocracoke Inlet.

Insider Tip: Visit Teach's Hole Blackbeard Exhibit and Pirate Specialty Shop in Ocracoke. The Blackbeard Exhibit includes original art, a life-size likeness of Blackbeard, weapons and medical tools, as well as scale models of Blackbeard's ships, and you can view a short documentary on the life of the infamous pirate.

Civil War History … and another first

It's probably hard for most people to imagine that the beautiful barrier islands of the Outer Banks were once Civil War battlefields, but in fact, they were of critical strategic importance in the war. With their proximity to the mainland of North Carolina, as well as the Pamlico and Albemarle Sounds, whichever side controlled the Outer Banks would control the rest of the state. Hatteras Inlet was both the most well-traveled and most vulnerable of the inlets along the Outer Banks. In 1861, North Carolina joined the Confederacy. Fort Clark and Fort Hatteras were constructed at the southern end of Hatteras Island by Confederate soldiers and slaves to control access to the Pamlico Sound. The forts came under attack by Union forces in August of 1861, forcing the Confederate commander to surrender control of the forts. It was the Union's first victory of the war. President Abraham Lincoln was reportedly roused from sleep to receive the news and danced a jig in his nightshirt to celebrate!

Graveyard of the Atlantic

Known as the Graveyard of the Atlantic, the treacherous waters off the Outer Banks have claimed hundreds of ships over the years, continuing through World War II and beyond. In an attempt to help ships, navigate more safely, several lighthouses were constructed. Arguably the most famous, the Cape Hatteras Lighthouse, was completed in 1802. In 1874, the U.S. Lifesaving Service, which later became the U.S. Coast Guard, was founded, and a chain of seven lifesaving stations was built along the Outer Banks.

Insider Tip: Visit the Graveyard of the Atlantic Museum in Hatteras. The museum features family-friendly activities such as scavenger hunts, as well as exhibits on everything from diving and fishing to close-up looks at lighthouse beacons and ships' bells.

Yet Another First

In 1880, Coast Guardsman Richard Etheridge became the first African American lifesaving station keeper when he was appointed to his post on Pea Island. In 1896, he led a crew of six in a daring rescue mission to save the crew of the E.S. Newman, a schooner that ran aground in a treacherous storm. In 2011, the Coast Guard launched the USCGC Richard Etheridge, an Island-class 110-foot patrol boat, to honor him.

A Breakthrough for All Mankind

One of the most profound events in Outer Banks history, as well as in the history of mankind, was the first successful manned flight on December 17, 1903, in what is now Kill Devil Hills. Most history books name the place of man's first flight as Kitty Hawk, because that was the nearest established town at the time. The Wright Brothers came to choose Kitty Hawk after receiving a letter from Octave Chanute, an aviation pioneer, who recommended the consistent breezes and soft sandy landing areas of the east coast for their flight trials. The location was narrowed to Kitty Hawk after the brothers received meteorological information on the area. In addition, in the remote location of the Outer Banks, the brothers could avoid the reporters that had hounded previous attempts at flight. As a result of their success, the entire state of North Carolina laid claim to being "First in Flight," a slogan seen on license plates, the name of a high school, an adventure park in Nags Head, and a multitude of other entities.

> *If we all worked on the assumption that what is accepted as true is really true, there would be little hope of advance. - Orville Wright*

On March 2, 1927, President Calvin Coolidge signed legislation authorizing the construction of a monument in Kill Devil Hills to commemorate the historic achievement of the Wright Brothers. Five years later, in 1932, the 60-foot granite monument was dedicated. The monument also acknowledges Icarus, a character from Greek mythology who sought to fly by attaching feathers to his arms with wax, as well as pays tribute to some of the early aviators who inspired the Wright Brothers. The ceremony dedicating the monument was attended by Orville Wright himself. (Wilbur Wright had passed away in 1912.)

The revolving beacon at the peak of the monument was continuously lit until World War II, when evening blackouts became mandatory. A few years later, the light was damaged in a storm. For 50 years, the Wright Brothers Memorial light was dark. In 1998, the light was restored to service.

The Wright Brothers National Memorial is open year-round, except for Christmas Day.

Preserving nature's beauty

The Cape Hatteras National Seashore was authorized by Congress on August 17, 1937, and established on January 12, 1953, with funds donated by Paul Mellon, heir to the Mellon Bank fortune and renowned breeder of racehorses. The area stretches some 70 miles, from Bodie Island to Ocracoke Island, and is managed by the National Park Service.

So, there you have it, a very brief introduction to the history of the Outer Banks. You can learn much more when you visit some of the attractions you'll find listed throughout this book.

Chapter 2 - The Beach Road

When vacationers drive across the Wright Memorial Bridge into Kitty Hawk, the first thing many people look for is that wonderful set of highway signs directing traffic to turn left toward Southern Shores, Duck, and Corolla or proceed straight ahead for Kitty Hawk, Kill Devil Hills, Nags Head, Manteo, and the Cape Hatteras National Seashore. You've arrived!

Most of this book will cover the towns of Kitty Hawk, Kill Devil Hills, and Nags Head, so I would recommend proceeding east on Route 158. After rounding the curve to the right — you'll see the Outer Banks Visitors Bureau — you will be on what the locals call The Bypass, which runs parallel to Route 12, known as the Beach Road. To get to the Beach Road, take a left at any point.

Insider Tip: If you decide to take a sharp left turn and explore the northern beaches, be aware that, at the time of publication, there is only one two-lane road heading north to Corolla, and during the summer vacation season, heavy traffic can cause a 40-minute drive to become a 2-hour drive — or worse.

For purposes of this chapter, however, since I promised you a drive down the Beach Road, we'll stay in the second-from-the-left lane, bear left, and then bear right onto North Virginia Dare Trail, yet another name for the Beach Road.

Kitty Hawk

There is disagreement about how Kitty Hawk got its name. Some say that Kitty Hawk is a Native American word for a place to hunt geese. Others claim it's an old English word for dragonfly. Regardless, Kitty Hawk is a lovely little town inhabited more by old growth trees and traditional beach cottages than anything else.

We adopted a kitty from Kitty Hawk, which seems appropriate, right? There is a wonderful group of people at a place called Feline Hope who not only help find homes for homeless cats, they also provide low-cost spay and neuter services, as well as rabies vaccinations. I highly recommend you consider them when making your charitable donations.

Beginning our journey down the beach road, the Hilton Garden Inn will be on your left, a big beautiful hotel adjacent to the Kitty Hawk Pier, where many a wedding takes place. My son married his lovely bride there. To your right you'll see the famous Duck Donuts — a can't-miss stop for at least one breakfast on your trip — and High Cotton Barbeque, featuring Eastern North Carolina-style pulled pork, Texas-style brisket, and fried chicken. Don't skip the hushpuppies!

Insider Tip: Eastern Carolina barbecue uses a "whole hog" method of chopping and mixing together almost all parts of the pig. The sauce is thin and vinegar-and-pepper-based, rather than tomato-based.

Our next stop on the Beach Road is the Rundown Cafe, a family-oriented, island-themed restaurant serving Caribbean and Pacific Rim dishes. You'll see it on the right as we travel south.

Much of the Beach Road in Kitty Hawk is inhabited only by beach houses. It's fun to see the different styles. In many places, you can enjoy a beautiful view of the ocean as you drive along, and you'll notice some empty lots where the sea has taken back the beach.

Around Milepost 2.5, on the corner of Eckner Street, is Ocean Boulevard Bistro & Martini Bar, another can't-miss destination. We held my daughter-in-law's bachelorette party there. When the weather is warm, you can enjoy your martini on their patio while listening to the soothing sounds of the ocean, as well as some live music. Be sure to order a bowl of stuffed olives!

Next on the right is Art's Place, just on the other side of Eckner Street. Laying claim to the "best burger on the beach," Art's also serves breakfast and offers a full-service bar and daily Happy Hour specials.

Right next to Art's Place is Muse Originals. This former firehouse turned art gallery showcases more than 75 local artists. You'll find handmade gifts, hand blown glass, jewelry, clothing, and more. Definitely not your run-of-the-mill souvenir shop!

Just past Muse Originals is Saltaire Cottages. They offer cottages from one to four bedrooms, each with a fully equipped kitchen, family room, and screen porch.

Coming up next on the right is the Sea Kove Motel, featuring small motor court style accommodations, nice for a weekend getaway, right across the street from the beach.

After we pass the Sea Kove, the Beach Road is mostly populated by beach houses until you reach the intersection with Kitty Hawk Road, where you'll see Hurricane Mo's Beachside Bar and the Black Pelican Oceanfront Restaurant. Hurricane Mo's is a lively, fun place, colorfully decorated, with great food and an outside deck. The Black Pelican is a delightful mix of elegant and comfortable. The food is so good that Guy Fieri once visited to tape a segment of his show *Diners, Drive-Ins, and Dives*. More importantly, however, it's where my husband and I celebrated our 28th wedding anniversary!

Continuing our drive south, we come to John's Drive-In, known and loved by OBX regulars. John's first opened in 1977 and is known for their amazing thick milkshakes, soft-serve ice cream, and everything from seafood subs to cheeseburgers. Your food is made to order. It gets crowded in the summer, but it's well worth the wait. Eat at one of their picnic tables or take your food across the street to the beach.

Insider Tip: Instead of getting fries with your meal, substitute an order of fried mushrooms. They're amazing!

Kill Devil Hills

Kill Devil Hills is the most populous town on the Outer Banks. Like its neighbor, Kitty Hawk, much lore surrounds the question of how the town got its name. The story officially endorsed by the town is that the origin of the name can be traced to a rum-carrying ship that ran aground on the beach. According to legend, locals scavenged the wreck and hid bottles of rum in the dunes. It was said that the rum was so strong that it could kill the devil. Thus, the dunes became known as Kill Devil Hills.

As we roll south on the Beach Road, one of the first landmarks you will see in Kill Devil Hills is the Avalon Pier on your left. Here you can fish, enjoy a cold beer, or play arcade games. They even have a live "pier-cam" so you can experience the beach anytime, even after your vacation is over.

Right across the street from the Avalon Pier is Awful Arthur's Oyster Bar. This is truly one of my favorite places on the Outer Banks. I'm no foodie, so there may be some who will disagree, but I think their steamed shrimp are the best of the beach. We rarely make a trip to the Outer Banks without dropping in at Arthur's.

Insider tip: This restaurant gets super-crowded during the summer, so your best bet is to go at an off time. We usually try to get a place at the bar. We frequently make a new friend or two while we're there, and the bar staff is always friendly. If you just want to stop in for a quick bite and a cold beer, I recommend the tuna bites or the crab dip — or both.

Continuing south, the Driftin' Sands Motel is on the right. It's an old school motor court type hotel that's great for a weekend getaway, when you just need the basics. All rooms have Wi-Fi, and some have kitchens.

Just past 4th Street, you'll see the Jolly Roger Restaurant on the right. It's a favorite among both locals and tourists for breakfast, but they're also open for lunch and dinner, as well. If you're into karaoke, this is your place, starting every night at 9:00 p.m. (10:00 p.m. on Fridays). The Jolly Roger is another of those places that can get crowded, especially during breakfast hours.

Insider tip: If yours is a smaller party of two or three, try the full-service bar. Often you can find seats there even when there's a long wait for a table, and you can order anything off the menu. Be sure to order a loaf (or two) of their fresh-baked bread to take with you!

Just down the street from the Jolly Roger, at 3rd Street, is the Days Inn & Suites Kill Devil Hills - Mariner. It's a good place for a night or long weekend when you just need a place to sleep and shower.

Next door to the Days Inn is the Sea Ranch Resort. The Sea Ranch is one of my top three choices for a fabulous view of the ocean. The balconies are large, with plenty of room to relax and gaze at the water. Also available are 2-bedroom/2-bath condos that include a full kitchen, a living room, and a double-length balcony. At the Sea Ranch, you have easy access to the beach, as well as umbrellas and chairs available for rent. There's a bar and restaurant on the first floor, and last time we stayed there, we received complimentary meal tickets for breakfast.

Insider Tip: The Sea Ranch often has some really good off-season deals, so be sure to sign up for their email newsletter so you'll be the first to know about them.

As we continue south on the Beach Road, the colorful sign for Goombays Grille & Raw Bar is hard to miss on the right-hand side. Located at Milepost 7, they have a wonderful seafood selection and offer a late-night steamed and raw bar menu until 2:00 a.m.

About a half-mile south of Goombays, just past Ferris Avenue, is the Travelodge Outer Banks. It's both budget-friendly as well as pet-friendly. Take note, however, that the beach in that area tends to get very crowded in the summer. In addition to the hotel, Ferris Avenue is a public access area with both a parking lot and street parking.

Just down the street is the Cypress House Inn, a five-room bed and breakfast. It makes for a nice change of pace from your run-of-the-mill motel room, and they even provide towels, umbrellas, and chairs to use at the beach.

Right across the street from the Cypress House Inn is the Quality Inn Carolina Oceanfront. This budget-friendly oceanfront hotel is great for a weekend getaway.

A couple of streets south of the Quality Inn is Wright Cottage Court, which offers a couple dozen cottages of various sizes (and prices), some of them oceanfront, all of them with fully equipped kitchens, available for nightly or weekly rental.

Just south of Wright Cottage Court, on the left, is the Days Inn Kill Devil Hills Oceanfront - Wilbur. It features a charming lobby with a wood-burning fireplace and cozy leather couches.

Continuing south, you'll see the Best Western Ocean Reef Suites on your left. It's definitely a step above your basic hotel. As the name implies, all the rooms are suites, and many of them are oceanfront.

Right next door to the Best Western is a nondescript little building that houses Outer Banks Bicycle. Both adult and children's bikes are available for rent, as well as kayaks, paddleboards, and surfboards. You can also rent beach chairs and umbrellas.

Pirates Beachwear is next on the left, and then we come to Shutters on the Banks, also on the left. Shutters is a unique beachfront hotel with 86 rooms, including oceanfront suites, as well as an indoor heated pool.

Across the street from Shutters is Secret Island Tavern, formerly known as Port O'Call. If you're looking for something different or a place to enjoy the nightlife, stop in at Secret Island. Tuesdays are comedy night, Wednesdays are reggae night, and any night of the week you can find live entertainment, a DJ, or karaoke. Or you can just hang out and shoot some pool.

On the other side of the street is Cavalier by The Sea, offering rooms, efficiencies, and cottages right on the beach. With no dunes to block your view, you can gaze at the ocean to your heart's content, or step off the porch for a short walk to the water's edge.

Continuing south, First Flight Retreat Condos are on the left. These oceanfront condos feature one, two, or three bedrooms and you can enjoy breathtaking ocean views and sunrises from your balcony. They also offer on-site paddleboard and kayak rentals, as well as a game room and fitness room. Some units even have private hot tubs.

The Outer Banks Beach Club Resort is next on the left as we continue our drive. With its clusters of round buildings, it's hard to miss. They offer one-, two-, and three-bedroom suites with fully equipped kitchens, plus both indoor and outdoor pools and a tennis court.

If you decide to stay at the Outer Banks Beach Club, you'll be within walking distance of Dare Devil's Pizzeria. Their dough and sauce are made fresh daily, in-house. Try one of their unique specialty pizzas or create your own. They also offer stromboli, salads, subs, and more, and you can pair your meal with a soft drink, beer, wine, or a cocktail.

Not in the mood for pizza? Try the nearby Bonzer Shack, just past East Martin Street. They offer seafood, burgers, and sandwiches. Open all year, with live entertainment during the summer.

Next on the right is a small strip shopping center. Businesses tend to come and go here, but one place that (so far) has stood the test of time is Food Dudes Kitchen. Billing itself as "a mellow eatery with a surf-shack vibe," Food Dudes offers fresh local seafood dishes with a Caribbean and Mexican flair. From sandwiches to quesadillas, plus wraps, burgers, and seafood entrees, there's something for everyone here.

Not far from Food Dudes is the See Sea Motel, which describes itself as being in "downtown" Kill Devil Hills. They offer standard rooms, as well as one- and two-bedroom apartments with full kitchens.

About three blocks further south, on the left, is the Outer Banks Motor Lodge, offering both oceanfront and poolside rooms and efficiencies. They are pet-friendly and within walking distance of Miller's Seafood & Steakhouse — our next stop on our Beach Road drive.

Miller's is open for breakfast from 7:00 a.m. till noon and for dinner starting at 4:00 p.m. Family-owned and operated, it's also right across the street from the Comfort Inn on the Ocean and the Ramada Plaza Nags Head Oceanfront. The Ramada, frankly, seems to have a bit of an identity crisis, since it's actually located in Kill Devil Hills, but I guess Nags Head has more name recognition. It has plenty of oceanfront rooms and is a good place for a weekend stay.

Continuing our drive, about two blocks farther south is the Kill Devil Grill. Originally known as Sam's Diner, it was built in 1940 by the Kullman Dining Car Company. It was moved to its current location in 1996 and in 1999 was listed in the National Register of Historic Places. I've never actually eaten there, because it's always super crowded. I've heard the food is great, and judging from the hour-long waits, I tend to believe it, but I recommend getting there before you're really hungry, because it could take a while to get a table.

Across the street from the Kill Devil Grill is the John Yancey Oceanfront Inn. At the time of publication, their website indicated that the hotel was undergoing renovation. The location is great, and they're pet-friendly!

As we continue south on the Beach Road, we will enter the Town of Nags Head. The last of the hotels in Kill Devil

Hills is TownePlace Suites by Marriott, on the right, and Seawalk Condominiums and Vacation Rentals on the left.

Nags Head

Nags Head is yet another town with an unusual name, one whose origin has been disputed over the years. There are several areas and establishments in the British Isles with the name Nag's Head, presumed by many to account for the town's name. According to folklore, however, the name is based on the practice of unscrupulous "wreckers" who would hang lanterns from the heads of horses in order to lure ships ashore, where they would wreck and be looted for their valuables.

As we come to the last of the Beach Road trilogy of towns, one of our first stops is in Gallery Row, at the Seagreen Gallery, on your right. All the souvenir and tee-shirt shops start to look the same after you've been to a few of them, and that's part of what makes Seagreen a welcome breath of fresh air. The shop is filled with repurposed and reclaimed artifacts that make unique and interesting gifts or great souvenirs for yourself. I like to use unusual containers for my flowers in the summer. One of my favorites is an old cast iron kettle I found at Seagreen. They also have lots of nautical items, driftwood, and seashells. You can buy yourself a big conch shell and tell people back home that you found it in Nags Head. (You won't be lying!) In the back is an outdoor area with a garden, birds, rabbits, and a goldfish pond.

Next door to Seagreen Gallery is Surfin' Spoon. Stop in for frozen yogurt, gelato, sorbet, or ice cream sandwich (made with scratch-baked cookies).

And right next door to Surfin' Spoon is Red Drum Grille & Taphouse, featuring fresh local seafood, steaks, ribs, and more. They offer 18 beers on tap, a game room, and video games, and serve bar food and steamed seafood until midnight.

At the next intersection, on the corner of Abalone Street, is Farmdog Surf School. They offer everything from set-up service for beach equipment to private and group surf lessons and equipment rentals. Next door is Something Fishy Gifts, an unusual gift shop offering home decor and clothing, among many other things. Nearby Gulf Stream Gifts sells fine jewelry and fashion jewelry with a beach theme, as well as t-shirts and souvenirs.

Just past East Admiral Street is Booty Treats Ice Cream & Shave Ice, boasting the "Best Booty on the Beach!" There's no denying — it's a great name. If you're looking for a refreshing treat or a fun dessert, this is your place. Their menu features everything from old-fashioned sundaes to Hawaiian shave ice to gourmet handmade ice cream cookie you're on vacation!

A couple of blocks south of Booty Treats is Seaside Art Gallery, established back when the Outer Banks was a remote and undeveloped area. Here you will find paintings, sculptures, and other pieces produced by local artists, as well as artists from around the world. Seaside is one of the largest art galleries in the southeast. The owner is an accredited appraiser and guarantees the authenticity of each piece.

A little farther down the road is Tortugas' Lie, a seafood restaurant with a Caribbean flair. Tortugas' Lie was another of Guy Fieri's stops when filming his Outer Banks segments for his show *Diners, Drive-Ins, and Dives*. If you're there during the off-season, stop in on Wednesday night for fresh sushi.

Another couple of blocks to the south is Lucky 12 Tavern. With a full lineup of sports channels, it's a fun and comfortable place to cheer on your favorite team. Their menu includes everything from local seafood to pizza — something for everyone. They offer 20 beers on tap, another 90 beers by the can or bottle, plus wine, martinis, and a full-service cocktail bar.

As we continue our trek southward, we come to the Nags Head Fishing Pier and Pier House Restaurant. Hang out and fish, then have the restaurant clean and cook your catch, serving it up fried, grilled, blackened, or broiled — complete with hushpuppies, coleslaw, and fries. Capt. Andy's Oceanfront Tiki Bar & Grill features live entertainment seven days a week during the season, with 30 beers on tap, specialty drinks, a full dinner menu, and fantastic views.

Just across from the pier is T-Shirt Whirl, where you can custom design your own t-shirt, tank top, or hoodie. You'll also find souvenirs and beach supplies, as well as the OBX Pirate Store.

Next on our drive, you'll see Snow Bird Burgers & Cones on the right. They feature soft serve ice cream, sundaes, and snow cones, plus a full menu for a casual lunch or dinner, with everything from dogs and burgers to seafood boats and sandwiches.

Just past Conch Street on the right is one of the five Brew-Thru locations in the Outer Banks. Brew-Thru gives new meaning to the term "convenience" store. You never have to leave your car. Just drive in and give your order to one of the "bartenders." They offer over 120 brands of beer, plus wine and other beverages, snacks, ice, and lots more.

Right next door to Brew-Thru is Austin Seafood Company. It's hard to miss the giant shark on the roof! If you're looking for fresh seafood to cook up, look no further. Austin's has anything you could possibly want to satisfy your seafood craving — clams, crabs, crab legs, lobster, scallops, shrimp of all sizes; tuna, salmon, shark, swordfish, and mahi mahi steaks; flounder, red snapper, grouper, tilapia, bluefish, and sea trout fillets. Don't feel like cooking? Austin's will cook it up for you, from individual meals to steamer buckets to feed a crowd.

If you're more in the mood for barbecue or ribs, Sooey's BBQ & Rib Shack is your place, and they're just a bit farther down the Beach Road, on your right. They feature hand-pulled eastern North Carolina style barbecue and hickory smoked ribs, plus fried chicken and buffalo wings.

Just past Sooey's is Jockey's Ridge Crossing shopping center. Here you will find the Life Is Good store, Kitty Hawk Kites, The Fudgery, Kitty Hawk Surf Co., and the Natural Life store.

Next door to Jockey's Ridge Crossing is The Old Nags Head Cafe, housed in a historic beach road grocery store. It's a favorite for breakfast, lunch, and dinner. It has a beachy feel with a touch of class and serves up contemporary southern cuisine, as well as local seafood.

As we continue south, at the corner of East Soundside Road on your right is Mulligan's Grille. Long known as the place to go for the "best burger on the beach," it's also a great place for local seafood. Mulligan's prides itself on being environmentally friendly, recycling everything from frying oil to oyster shells, and they are one of the few restaurants in the Outer Banks that's open 365 days a year.

Traveling another couple of blocks to the south, we come to the Cavalier Surf Shop on the right. This is one of the original stores in Nags Head, dating back to the 1960s. Offering a variety of surf and skate equipment, they also carry beach gear and novelties. Want to give surfing or paddle-boarding a try without making a big investment? Cavalier has rental equipment, too.

Just ahead on the left is the Holiday Inn Express Nags Head (formerly the Nags Head Inn). I've always liked the Holiday Inn Express chain and would probably recommend it for that reason alone. But because of its great ocean views, I've put it in my Top Three best oceanfront hotels. In addition, it's located in a quiet area where the beach doesn't get too crowded.

Several blocks to the south are the Windjammer Resort, rental condominiums with easy access to the beach. Each two-bedroom/two-bath unit is fully furnished, with well equipped kitchens.

If your drive down the Beach Road has you ready for a treat, stop in at Scammell's Corner Surf Shop & Ice Cream Parlor. This family-owned combo business, as the name suggests, sells both ice cream and surfboards. They also have surfboards available for rent, as well as surf lessons. In addition, they offer paddle boards, boogie boards, beach equipment, clothing, and souvenirs.

Next, we have a series of motels. The SandSpur Ocean Cottages is on the left as we continue our drive. Then you'll see the Surf Side Hotel, offering oceanfront rooms, efficiencies, and suites. The Blue Heron Motel is located in the next block. One nice feature of the Blue Heron is that all their rooms face the ocean. The next motel is the Islander, also on the left, and then the Tar Heel Motel, on the right. According to the Tar Heel website, they are "completely renovated" and "100% remodeled."

Next, on the left, is the Sea Foam Motel. If you're looking for accommodations with an authentic retro beach feel, the Sea Foam is the place to stay. It's listed in the National Register of Historic Places and is a refreshing change from the cookie-cutter style of many of the chain hotels. Whether you choose an oceanfront or poolside room, you'll feel right at home at the Sea Foam. Staying there reminded me of a motel we frequently stayed at when I was a child. It was called the Surf & Sands, located in Ocean City, Maryland.

Owens' Restaurant is right across the street from the Sea Foam and is another good choice if you're in the mood for a fresh local seafood dinner.

Next on the right is OBX Toy Rentals. Here you can rent a low-speed vehicle (LSV) or a scoot coupe. It can come in handy if your vacation rental is more than a block or two from the beach. They also have a variety of types of bicycles available for rent, as well as scooters.

Fatboyz Ice Cream comes up next on the right. Not only do they have an assortment of ice cream treats, they also offer sandwiches, boats, hot dogs, and burgers.

Cahoons Cottages and Market is next on the left. They have about a dozen cottages for rent, ranging from efficiencies to four bedrooms. The market offers everything from fresh meat to wine.

Cahoons is right next door to Jennette's Pier. In addition to it being a great place to fish, you can also explore interactive science exhibits. Fishing gear is available for rent, and they also have beach supplies and snacks.

Sam & Omie's, next on our right, is one of those places people will tell you is a "must" when you visit the Outer Banks. It started as a place for fishermen to get breakfast before they headed out for the day and has grown to be a very popular stop not only for breakfast but for lunch and dinner, as well.

Rounding the corner, as the Beach Road turns slightly west, you'll see Dune Burger on your right. If you're a fan of *American Idol*, you may remember the young man with the very deep voice, Scotty McCreery. In 2014, he made a video for his song *Feelin' It*, and Dune Burger was briefly featured. They offer typical beach food — hot dogs, fries, and ice cream — and of course, burgers.

That's pretty much it for the "good ole Beach Road." Lots of places to stay and play or stop and eat. Just before you get to Dune Burger, if you bear to the left, you can continue on Rt. 1243, more commonly known as South Old Oregon Inlet Road. This area features mostly vacation cottages, but there are a few hotels, and it's worth heading down that way to the Outer Banks Fishing Pier, where you can enjoy 15-cent shrimp and a cold beer at Fish Heads Bar and Grill.

Insider Tip: As you enjoy your drive down the beach road, be courteous to pedestrians and remember that they always have the right of way in crosswalks. If you see a person or group of people waiting to cross, stop at the crosswalk and let them pass.

But what if I just want to go to the beach?

I know what you're thinking. It's called the Beach Road. How do I just get to the beach? No worries. I've got you covered.

I like anywhere with a beach. A beach and warm weather are all I really need. — Rob Gronkowski

All along the Beach Road, you will see public beach access signs. In addition to parking lots, many of these areas have showers and porta-potties. In Chapter 4, I've listed the ones that are more than just a place where you're allowed to walk over the dunes, and I identify areas where there are handicap access points, wooden walkways, and lifeguards. Keep in mind that, during the busy season, the parking lots tend to be full by 10 a.m.

So, that's the end of our virtual drive down the Beach Road, but it's far from all that Rt. 12 has to offer. Continue the drive to visit the Bodie Island Lighthouse, spend the day at Coquina Beach, check out the Oregon Inlet Marina, or head across the newly constructed Basnight Bridge, which replaces the 50-year-old Bonner Bridge, to visit the towns of the southern Outer Banks, including the famous Cape Hatteras Lighthouse, and take a ride — car and all — on the ferry to Ocracoke. You will also find more detailed information on Beach Road accommodations, restaurants, and attractions in the chapters that follow.

Chapter 3 - Vacation Rentals

Planning a summer vacation in the Outer Banks is exciting — and it's the perfect cure for the winter blues. But with hundreds of choices, it can be overwhelming deciding where to stay. In addition, for the first-time OBX vacationer — or maybe it's your first time doing the planning — there are many things to consider in order to make your vacation the most enjoyable — and avoid disappointments.

When my son and his now-wife decided to have their wedding in the Outer Banks, I wanted to rent an oceanfront beach house to provide accommodations for our friends and family. I also wanted to hold the rehearsal dinner there. My elderly father was confined to a wheelchair, so we needed an elevator. We had two dozen people coming to the rehearsal dinner, so we needed two large dining tables. In addition, there were other considerations that had to be taken into account. I actually made a spreadsheet to narrow my choices.

You, too, may also find it necessary to develop a systematic procedure to help you choose the perfect accommodations for your vacation. In this chapter, I provide some basic information and definitions to get you started.

Types of accommodations

There are basically three types of accommodations in the Outer Banks: campgrounds, hotels and motels, and rental houses.

Campgrounds

As previously mentioned, my idea of "roughing it" is a hotel room without a minibar, but I know lots of people love to camp, and if you're going to do it, I can't think of any better place than the Outer Banks. In the area covered by this book — Kitty Hawk/Kill Devil Hills/Nags Head — there aren't a lot of campgrounds. The majority of Outer Banks campgrounds are located south of Oregon Inlet and will be covered in volume two of this series. But here is a list of the ones located between Kitty Hawk and Nags Head.

The Preserve at Kitty Hawk Woods - This campground is for RVs only and leases on a year-round basis only. So, if you own an RV and want a permanent Outer Banks home away from home, this is a great place to set up. The quiet but convenient location makes it easy to get to the beach and nearby businesses, and with only 31 sites on 10 acres, you'll have plenty of privacy.

Location: 4352 The Woods Rd, Kitty Hawk, (252) 548-6102

Kitty Hawk RV Park - Wi-fi, full hookups, and dump station.

Location: 3945 North Croatan Highway (MP 4), Kitty Hawk, (252) 261-2636

OBX Campground - 56 RV sites, nightly and weekly rates, wi-fi, full hookups, guest laundry, and dump site.

Location: 126 Marshy Ridge Road, Kill Devil Hills, (252) 564-4741

Joe & Kay's Campground - A small campground with 10 sites, hot and cold water, and a boat ramp.

Location: 1193 Colington Road, Kill Devil Hills, (252) 441-5468

Oregon Inlet Campground - This is the northernmost of the Cape Hatteras National Seashore campgrounds. It features three bathhouses and heated outdoor showers. Each camping space has a paved parking pad, picnic table, and charcoal grill. Some campsites including RV hookups. A water-fill and dump station are available to campers at the Oregon Inlet Marina across the street. The beach is a short walk from the campground.

The Refuge on Roanoke Island - Located in the fishing village of Wanchese, this campground has 56 sites with full hookups. However, 44 of them are year-long leases, leaving only a dozen of them available for daily campers, so be sure to make your reservation early. Those 12 sites are all waterfront, perfect for catch-and-release fishing or crabbing.

Location: 2881 NC Highway 345, Wanchese, (252) 473-1096

Bed & Breakfasts

I personally have never stayed in a bed and breakfast, but if that's your style, there are several to choose from on the Outer Banks:

Cameron House Inn, 300 Budleigh Street, Manteo, (800) 279-8178

Cypress House Inn, 500 North Virginia Dare Trail, Kill Devil Hills, (252) 441-6127

Cypress Moon Inn, 1206 Harbor Court, Kitty Hawk, (252) 202-2731

RelaxInn Bed & Breakfast, 8008 S. Old Oregon Inlet Road, Nags Head, (252) 441-2202

Sandbar Bed & Breakfast, 2508 South Virginia Dare Trail, Nags Head, (252) 489-1868

Scarborough House Inn, 323 Fernando St, Manteo, (252) 473-3849

The White Doe Inn, 319 Sir Walter Raleigh Street, Manteo, (252) 473-9851

Hotels and Motels

OBX hotels and motels are best for vacationing couples who want the convenience of daily maid service and other hotel perks — or for short stays. Even during peak season, oceanfront rooms are available at a fraction of the cost of most oceanfront cottages, and if you're planning to stay for less than a week, hotels may be your only option.

Insider Tip: If you plan to stay for less than a week, check Airbnb. You may be able to rent a room or an entire cottage by the night, often for less than motel rates.

If proximity to the beach is important for you, definitely do your research to ensure you're going to be happy with your room. Just because a motel advertises itself as oceanfront does not necessarily mean your room will be oceanfront, and in fact, oceanfront can mean different things. There are hotels with fabulous oceanfront rooms (the Sea Ranch in Kill Devil Hills is one of them) and hotels where oceanfront could mean you have a large dune between you and the beach or only an indirect view of the water. If you want an oceanfront room, make sure you specify that when making your reservation. I've marked the hotels that, in my opinion, have the best oceanfront views with ⚓.

Beachwoods Resort
(252) 261-4610
1 Cypress Knee Trail
Kitty Hawk

Hilton Garden Inn Outer Banks
(252) 261-1290
5353 North Virginia Dare Trail (Beach Road)
Kitty Hawk

Saltaire Cottages
(833) 725-8247
4618 North Virginia Dare Trail (Beach Road)
Kitty Hawk

Baymont by Wyndham Kitty Hawk Outer Banks
(252) 261-4888
3919 North Croatan Highway
Kitty Hawk

Driftin' Sands Motel
1906 North Virginia Dare Trail (Beach Road)
Kill Devil Hills
(252) 715-4100

Days Inn & Suites Mariner
(252) 256-7412
1801 North Virginia Dare Trail (Beach Road)
Kill Devil Hills

⚓ Sea Ranch Resort
(252) 441-7126
1731 North Virginia Dare Trail (Beach Road MP 7)
Kill Devil Hills

Travelodge by Wyndham Outer Banks/Kill Devil Hills
804 N Virginia Dare Trail (Beach Road)
Kill Devil Hills
(252) 441-0411

Quality Inn Carolina Oceanfront
401 N. Virginia Dare Trail (Beach Road)
Kill Devil Hills
(252) 480-2600

Days Inn Oceanfront Wright Brothers
(800) 325-2525
201 North Virginia Dare Trail (Beach Road)
Kill Devil Hills

Best Western Ocean Reef Suites
(252) 441-1611
107 South Virginia Dare Trail (Beach Road)
Kill Devil Hills

Shutters on the Banks
(252) 441-5581
405 S Virginia Dare Trail (Beach Road)
Kill Devil Hills

Cavalier by The Sea
(252) 441-5584
601 S Virginia Dare Trail (Beach Road)
Kill Devil Hills

Outer Banks Inn
(888) 322-9702
1003 S Croatan Highway
Kill Devil Hills

Outer Banks Motor Lodge
(252) 441-7404
1509 South Virginia Dare Trail (Beach Road
Kill Devil Hills

Comfort Inn on the Ocean
(252) 441-6333
1601 South Virginia Dare Trail (Beach Road)
Kill Devil Hills

Ramada Plaza by Wyndham Nags Head Oceanfront
(252) 564-7222
1701 South Virginia Dare Trail (Beach Road)
Kill Devil Hills

John Yancey Inn
(252) 441-7141
2009 S. Virginia Dare Trail (Beach Road MP 10)
Kill Devil Hills

TownePlace Suites Outer Banks
(252) 457-2190
2028 South Virginia Dare Trail (Beach Road)
Kill Devil Hills

Colonial Inn
(252) 441-7308
3329 S Virginia Dare Trail (Beach Road)
Nags Head

Holiday Inn Express Nags Head Oceanfront
(252) 441-0454
4701 South Virginia Dare Trail (Beach Road)
Nags Head

Sandspur Motel & Cottage Court
(252) 441-6993
6607 South Virginia Dare Trail (Beach Road)
Nags Head

Surf Side Hotel
(800) 552-7873
6701 S Virginia Dare Trail (Beach Road)
Nags Head

First Colony Inn
(252) 441-2343
6715 South Croatan Highway
Nags Head

The Islander Motel
(252) 441-6229
7001 South Virginia Dare Trail (Beach Road)
Nags Head

Tar Heel Motel
(855) 842-2164
7010 South Virginia Dare Trail (Beach Road)
Nags Head

Owens Motel
(252) 441-6361
7115 South Virginia Dare Trail (Beach Road)
Nags Head

Comfort Inn South Oceanfront
(252) 441-6315
8031 Old Oregon Inlet Road (Beach Road)
Nags Head

Vacation Rental Homes

Location, location, location

The first thing you should do when starting your search for a vacation rental home is get familiar with the term's rental companies use in their catalogs and online listings to describe the location of the home.

Oceanfront is exactly what it sounds like. Your house will face the ocean and, depending on the height of the dunes relative to the house, you should have a good view. In general, oceanfront homes in Kitty Hawk will have the best views and easiest beach access. The farther south you go, the more likely that you will have a dune between your house and the beach. In Nags Head, almost all the homes have large dunes in front of them. Not only does a dune make accessing the beach more difficult, but in some cases, it can impede your view of the beach completely depending on how the house is constructed.

Insider Tip: Beach access can vary, depending on whether the owners have built a walkway from the house across the dunes. In a few cases, particularly in Kitty Hawk, you may find houses that do not have dunes in front of them, which leaves the homes more vulnerable but makes beach access a lot easier. If that's important to you, be sure to ask the rental company. Otherwise, keep in mind that the dunes can be a bit of a challenge to navigate, particularly without some type of walkway. If anyone in your party has mobility challenges, be sure to take this into account. It's also a good idea to ask if the walkway or stairs to the beach are clear of sand. This type of maintenance can vary, and particularly if there has been a recent storm, stairs and walkways can be completely covered in sand.

Oceanside means the house is on the east side of Route 12 (the Beach Road) but there will be another house between yours and the ocean. It may or may not have a view of the ocean, so be sure to check the description. Homes with an oceanside location are mostly found in Nags Head, where there are often two or three rows of houses between the beach and the beach road.

Semi-oceanfront can refer to a house that fronts Route 12 on the west side -- in other words, you'll have to cross the Beach Road to get to the beach -- or it can refer to houses on the east side of the Beach Road that have one house between it and the beach. In general, in Kitty Hawk and Kill Devil Hills, there is only one row of houses on the east side of the Beach Road. However, in Nags Head, it's not unusual to find two or three rows of houses on the beach side.

Insider Tip: If you rent an oceanfront or semi-oceanfront house, the views of the night sky can be spectacular on a clear night. If you're lucky enough — or plan well enough — to have a full moon during your stay, the moonrise is fantastic. When the sky is moonless, you'll see so many stars it's difficult to take them all in. It's also fairly common to see some shooting stars. If you have a telescope, be sure to bring it along. Also, please be considerate of your neighbors. Nothing ruins a beautiful view of the stars quicker than a powerful flood light. Turn your outside lights off when you don't need them, particularly the ones on the ocean side, so others can enjoy the view of the sky.

Between-the-highway houses are situated between Route 12 and Route 58 (the Bypass). They may be as many as three or four blocks back from the Beach Road.

Soundfront or *soundside* means the house will be located on the Albemarle Sound on the west side of the island.

Canalfront refers to a house located on one of the many canals on the west side of the island.

Insider Tip: There is an area of Kill Devil Hills known as Colington Island. It's located where Albemarle Sound, Currituck Sound, Croatan Sound, and Roanoke

Sound all converge. Although it's referred to as one island, it's actually two separate islands, Big Colington and Little Colington. On Big Colington is the gated community of Colington Harbour. Many of the homes in Colington Harbour (as well as other parts of Colington) are available for seasonal rental. Colington Harbour is about 4 miles from the oceanfront along a fairly winding two-lane road, making it somewhat removed from the heart of Kill Devil Hills. It's definitely a boater's paradise, and there is a designated swimming area in the sound.

Things to consider in choosing a rental

The houses for rent in the Outer Banks range from 12-bedroom estates with peak season weekly rents in the 5 figures to 1-bedroom bungalows you can rent for less than $1,000 per week. The difference in price between an oceanfront location and an oceanside location is dramatic, as much as 75% more for an oceanfront house.

Most rental houses have a variety of sleeping accommodations — from king-size beds to bunk beds. Many of the larger, more expensive houses have a private bath for each bedroom, and some have either two separate kitchens or an extra-large kitchen, sometimes with two ranges and two dishwashers, which is great for large groups. In all cases, kitchens come fully equipped with dishes and cookware. You can also find houses with a separate, stand-alone icemaker, hot tub (sometimes more than one), pool table, theater room, and in-ground pool. Most have outside showers.

All of these houses are built on pilings, which means there are stairs, sometimes lots and lots of stairs. Most have reverse floor plans, with the kitchen and living area on the top floor and the bedrooms on a lower floor, making it likely you'll be hauling your groceries up at least one set of stairs. Some houses have elevators, so if you'll be traveling with someone who has mobility issues, it may be worth the extra cost.

Insider Tip: **If at all possible, I recommend making a reconnaissance trip before selecting a rental. Plan a weekend to drive around and look at the houses you're considering. If the house is vacant, the realty company may let you have a key so you can go inside and look around. Or — don't tell anyone I told you this — you can walk up on the deck to see the view and maybe peek in the windows. (Again, don't do this unless it's obvious the house is unoccupied.)**

Vacation Rental Companies

Airbnb
Beach Realty - (800) 635-1559
Brindley Beach Vacations & Sales - (877) 642-3224
Carolina Designs - (800) 368-3825
Elan Vacations - (800) 458-3830
First Flight Rentals - (866) 595.1893
Joe Lamb, Jr. - (800) 552-6257
Resort Realty - (800) 458-3830
Sea Spray Cottages - (804) 337.7850
Seaside Vacations - (800) 395-2525
Southern Shores Realty - (800) 334-1000
Stan White Realty - (800) 338-3233
Sun Realty - (888) 853-7770
Twiddy - (866) 457-1190
VRBO
Village Realty - (800) 441-8533
Wright Cottage Court - (252) 441-7331

Reserve early!

The best homes get snagged early, so if you're planning a vacation for peak season (from mid-June to late August), don't wait! If you put off making your reservation, you may end up disappointed.

What to bring

Obviously, what you're able to pack may depend on whether you're driving or flying. Be sure to bring the typical essentials: medications, diapers, chargers for electronics, and toiletries (including soap, since beach rentals do not provide these items). You should also bring at least one roll of toilet paper for each bathroom, as well as a roll of paper towels and trash bags. You can stock up on everything the day after you arrive, but make sure you have enough to get you through the first evening and the next morning.

Most vacation rentals offer the option of renting linens and some will make up the beds for you before your arrival. In addition, cribs are usually available.

Insider Tip: If you need a crib, check on availability when you reserve your home. If your rental company offers the option of making the beds for you before you arrive, take advantage of it. No matter where you're traveling from, it's likely that the day of your arrival will be a long one, and it's great to not have to worry about making the beds.

Many vacation homes have beach toys such as buckets and boogie boards on hand. At some houses, you will also find beach chairs and other equipment. However, these types of items are usually not guaranteed. So, if you have your own beach equipment and you have available space in your vehicle, plan to bring your own. If, however, you're arriving by air, don't want to buy a bunch of beach stuff for a one-week vacation, or you don't have the room (or the inclination, perhaps) to pack everything in your vehicle, you may want to look into renting equipment.

Insider Tip: You can rent just about anything you need for your vacation stay. From basics such as beach chairs and umbrellas to bicycles and kayaks, you can reserve what you need in advance and have it delivered to your beach house. Some companies even offer a beach set-up service, so all you have to do is make your way to the beach and relax.

Food

Be sure to consider food for the first night and first morning of your stay. With most vacation rentals, check-in time is 4:00 p.m. By the time you get the key to your house and haul in all your stuff, you'll probably find yourself wondering what to do about dinner. I recommend preparing something ahead of time to bring with you or pick up something before you check in. Believe me, after traveling all day and schlepping all your luggage and supplies into your beach house, you're going to be tired and your kids will probably be cranky. The last thing you'll want to do is turn around and head back out to find a restaurant (where you may have to wait an hour to get a table) or go to the grocery store, then come back and cook dinner. Plan ahead for both dinner the night of your arrival and breakfast the next day. (Consider ordering in for dinner. See below for a list of local restaurants that deliver.) Don't forget to bring coffee, coffee filters, sweetener, creamer, and milk for cereal! You'll probably want to bring along some bottled water or other beverages, as well as snacks, too. Our practice is usually to make a trip to the grocery store mid-morning on Sunday.

Restaurants that deliver

At time of publication, neither GrubHub nor DoorDash was serving the Outer Banks. However, there are several restaurants that will deliver to your vacation rental, and you're not limited to just pizza. You can even get beer and wine delivered!

Max's Italian Restaurant - Salads, pizza, stromboli, calzones, pasta, subs, paninis, and desserts. Call: 252-261-3113

Country Deli - If you love a good sandwich, you'll love the Country Deli. Try one of their "Famous Pounders," a Triple-Decker, one of a dozen other specialty sandwiches or a classic deli sandwich. They also have vegetarian choices, salads, and grilled cheese. Call: (252) 441-5684

Slice Pizzeria - Not just pizza. They also have salads, subs, calzones, stromboli, pasta, and desserts. Call: (252) 449-8888

Colington Pizza - If you're staying in Colington, they will be happy to deliver to you. Build your own pizza or stromboli, or order a sub, sandwich, or salad. Call: (252) 441-3339

Sal's New York Pizza - Sandwiches, salads, hot and cold subs, pasta, and of course, pizza. Call: (252) 715-3145

Nags Head Pizza Company - Specialty pizzas and build-your-own salads. Call: (252) 715-3455

Pizzazz Pizza - Delivering pizza, of course, and also wings, salads, and subs. Call: (252) 261-1111

South Beach - Bowls, wraps, sandwiches, cheesesteaks, burgers, salads, and even selections for your furry family member. Call: (252) 255-1698

Domino's Pizza - If you're a fan of Domino's, you're in luck! (Pretty sure they will even bring it out to the beach for you if you want!) Call: (252) 441-1525

Pizza Hut - For fans of The Hut, you can have all your favorites delivered. Call: (252) 441-7101

Papa John's - Can't live without the garlic dipping sauce? PJ's has you covered at the beach. Call: (252) 261-2389

Groceries

As mentioned in the Introduction, there was a time when vacationers had to bring enough groceries to last throughout their time in the OBX. Those days are long gone. There are a number of chain grocery stores between Kitty Hawk and Nags Head, including several Food Lion stores, a Super Walmart, Harris Teeter, Publix, and Fresh Market.

Insider Tip: Publix in Kill Devil Hills offers online shopping. You can pick up your order or have it delivered. Be sure to put in your order a couple of days ahead of time to ensure you can reserve the pickup or delivery time you want.

Keep in mind that the Outer Banks is a resort area, and prices are generally higher. So, if you're able to load up on some staples — such as paper goods, for example — you may want to pick those up ahead of time.

Insider Tip: If you'll be vacationing with a group, such as extended family, consider creating a list of items all of you will be using, like hand soap, condiments, and toilet paper, then assign people to bring specific things. Not only does it help to spread the cost more evenly, but it helps avoid the possibility of ending up with 14 rolls of paper towels but only 4 rolls of toilet paper.

One great thing about buying groceries in the OBX stores is you will find a good selection of the kinds of things vacationers want: meats, beer and wine, beach supplies, and souvenirs.

Insider Tip: One of the first things you want to do when you get into your rental house is check the refrigerator to make sure it hasn't been turned off. This is common if the house wasn't occupied the week before. When you turn up the temperature, stop shy of cranking it up all the way. Some refrigerators tend to freeze everything inside if you turn it up too high. Also — this is important — DO NOT load $400 worth of groceries into the fridge the moment you arrive. It could take 24 hours or more for it to cool off if you overload it with a bunch of warm cans of soda and other items that don't absolutely have to be refrigerated. Instead, put your canned and bottled beverages in a cooler. Some rental houses have separate ice makers, often found on the lower level of the house, and if not, there's a store selling ice on almost every corner.

Fresh Seafood

A seafood feast is something we always look forward to on an Outer Banks vacation. Steamed shrimp, grilled tuna steaks, and pan seared scallops — makes my mouth water just thinking about it!

Carawan Seafood Company - You'll find Carawan's just after you come across the Wright Memorial Bridge, on the right-hand side. It's locally owned and specializes in local fish and shellfish. They also carry a selection of seasonal vegetables, wine and beer, gourmet foods, and fishing tackle. They're open year-round.

Location: 5424 North Croatan Highway, Kitty Hawk, (252) 261-2120

Austin Fish Company - Austin's is near Jockey's Ridge, and is our go-to place for fresh seafood. You will find every type of seafood you could possibly want, from several sizes of shrimp to scallops, tuna steaks, flounder, mahi mahi, and salmon. In the mood for clams or crabs? They have a variety of both. Take your purchase back to your vacation rental to cook or have Austin's cook it for you. Feeding a crowd? Order a couple of steamer buckets that feed up to six people each and include the main course plus all the fixins!

Location: 3711 South Croatan Highway (Bypass MP 12.5), Nags Head, (252) 441.7412

Insider Tip: Call ahead to be sure you can get your order steamed or fried up fresh and hot when you want it.

Whalebone Seafood - Locally sourced seafood and knowledgeable staff who can help you make your selection and give you tips on how to prepare it. They have every type of seafood you could want, plus all the fixins. Call ahead to have your order steamed and ready for pickup.

Location: 101 Grey Eagle Street, (off the Bypass MP 16.5), Nags Head, (252) 441-8808

O'Neal's Sea Harvest - For the very best fresh local seafood, O'Neal's is worth straying off the beaten path. They purchase locally caught seafood daily. Yellowfin tuna, croaker, red drum, bluefish, black sea bass, and flounder are available year-round. Wahoo and mahi mahi is available during the summer months. They also offer soft shell crabs, blue crabs, shrimp, and scallops in season. If you've never had truly fresh — *yesterday it was swimming!* — seafood, you're in for a great treat. O'Neal's will even prepare and pack a cooler for you to take home. Not in the mood to cook? Drop in for lunch and enjoy a variety of menu items made to order.

Location: 622 Harbor Road, Wanchese, NC, (252) 473-4535

Billy's Seafood - Locally owned and in operation for nearly 50 years, Billy's has a wide selection of seafood and will steam your crabs and have them hot and ready for pickup.

Location: 1341 Colington Road, Kill Devil Hills, (252) 441-5978

Sugar Shack Seafood Market - Located next door to Sugar Creek Seafood Restaurant, they offer fresh seafood and seafood prepared to order.

Location: 7340 South Virginia Dare Trail (Manteo Causeway), Nags Head, (252) 441-3888

Beer, Wine, and Liquor

In North Carolina, beer and wine can be purchased at any grocery store and is also sold in other types of stores, such as convenience stores, drug stores, and some souvenir shops. Liquor can be purchased only at a state-operated ABC store. There are two ABC store locations in the Kitty Hawk/Kill Devil Hills/Nags Head area:

5400 North Croatan Highway, Kitty Hawk, (252) 261-2477

This store is located on the right-hand side, after you cross the Wright Memorial Bridge. Turn right on Cypress Knee Trail.

2104 South Croatan Highway, Nags Head, (252) 441-5121

This store is at the intersection of the bypass and West 8th Street.

Insider Tip: You _cannot_ purchase alcohol in any location, including restaurants, before noon on Sundays.

Traveling

The majority of vacationers drive to the Outer Banks. The nearest major airport serving the Outer Banks is Norfolk International Airport, which is about 80 miles from the Wright Brothers Memorial Bridge. There is also the Newport News/Williamsburg International Airport, which is about 100 miles from the bridge.

Be warned: Summer traffic to the Outer Banks is brutal. If you are heading into the OBX from the north following the conventional route of VA-168 to NC-168 to NC-158 across the Wright Brothers Memorial Bridge, you can expect to have lots of company on the road.

My number one tip for avoiding the traffic is to leave early enough that you can get across the bridge before noon. This means you will have some time to kill before you can get into your vacation rental. Please refer to the section below for some ideas of what you can do to keep yourselves and/or your kids busy while you wait for check-in time. For an extra fee, some vacation rental companies will allow you to check in early.

Another way to avoid some of the traffic getting into the Outer Banks is to choose a Sunday-to-Sunday rental. For most vacation rentals, Saturday is the turnover day, meaning you can expect a lot of competition getting to and from the OBX on Saturdays. By arriving and departing on Sunday instead, you will miss the worst traffic day. Another option is to book a hotel room for Friday night. You will still have time to kill between check-out time at the hotel and check-in time for your vacation rental, but at least you'll already be there instead of fighting the Saturday afternoon traffic.

Insider Tip: This won't help you avoid the bridge traffic, but once you manage to make it into Kitty Hawk, you can take the second right onto The Woods Road. Follow it to Kitty Hawk Road, which will take you back out to Rt. 158 and help you get around a bit of the traffic.

If you're driving in from the west or south — or if you want to try an alternate route coming in from the north -- you can take US-64 into Manteo. Coming in from the north, take Exit 296 to US-17, then continue on US-17 to NC-37 across the Albemarle Sound and pick up US-64 to Manteo or follow I-95 South to US-64 to Manteo.

If all else fails, take your time, stop for lunch or other activities on your way, and purposely arrive later in the day. Peak times for summer traffic on Saturdays are between noon and 4:00 p.m. There are several things you can do along Rt. 158:

Border Station – As you travel along Rt. 168 in Virginia, approaching the North Carolina border, the Border Station will be on your right. It's kind of a fun little convenience store and souvenir shop. It's unique because the store itself is actually in both states. You can cross from one state into the other inside the store. My mother always loved to stop there when we traveled to the Outer Banks.

Powell's Roadside Market – About 10 miles further south is Powell's Roadside Market. They sell everything from fresh fruits and vegetables to homemade fudge. And they have restrooms! In the summer, there's usually lots of activity. It's a good place to stop and stretch your legs … and pick up a watermelon for your vacation!

Morris Farm Market – Another 8 miles down the road is Morris Farm Market. In addition to fresh fruits and vegetables, they also offer a variety of homemade baked goods, fresh roasted peanuts, and wine. They have a picnic area, and young and old alike will get a kick out of their vintage tractor collection.

Diggers Dungeon – If you're traveling with children, you will probably want to schedule Diggers Dungeon into your plans. It's about 8 miles past Morris Farm Market and is home to the world-famous Grave Digger monster truck. They usually have several monster trucks on display, including a vintage Grave Digger, and you can even take a ride on one! Stop in at Diggers Diner for lunch.

Weeping Radish Brewery – Continuing south for another 5 miles, the Weeping Radish Brewery is on your right. You can arrange ahead of time to take a tour of the brewery or just stop in for lunch at the pub. They recently changed their sign to read Weeping Radish Brewery and Charcuterie, so as you might expect, you can also pick up some fresh sausage, hot dogs, and other cold meats.

(Note: About a mile south of the Weeping Radish is the location of the Cotton Gin, on the left. At the time of publication, the Jarvisburg location has not yet been rebuilt following a fire in 2019.)

Lammers Glass Gifts & Antiques – Another 4 miles or so on the left you will come to Lammers. They feature beautiful hand-blown glass, stained glass, soaps, garden decor, and more. (If you decide to stop there on your way to the OBX, keep in mind that you will need to make a left turn back out onto the highway to continue to your destination. This can be a tricky proposition with the heavy traffic in the summer, so you may want to stop there on your way home *after* your stay on the Outer Banks.)

H2OBX Waterpark – Just 4 miles south of Lammers is H2OBX Waterpark. It's about 10 miles north of the Wright Memorial Bridge, so you're likely to experience some the heavy prime time traffic in the summer, but why not plan to stop there and begin your vacation early? If you get as far as H2OBX by early afternoon, you're still going to have time to kill before you can get into your rental, making this waterpark the perfect appetizer for your vacation, not to mention a great way to let your kids burn off some energy after being trapped in the car for hours.

What to do if you get there early

One of the tricky things about planning your travel is that, while it's best if you arrive as early as possible to avoid traffic, you won't be able to get into your rental cottage until late afternoon, so you'll want to have a plan for what to do in the meantime.

Insider Tip: Some realty companies will allow you to arrange for early arrival. You may have to pay an additional fee, but if you call them with an estimated time of arrival at some point while you're traveling, they may be willing to accommodate you. It's worth a try.

You can always plan to head right out to the beach to kill time. You may be able to find parking along a side street (pay attention to the no-parking signs) or find a space to park in a public access lot. Make sure you have plenty of sunscreen and cold drinks.

Insider Tip: In the summer, the sand can get extremely hot. It might be relatively cool if you head out to the beach before mid-morning, but there's a good chance it will be very hot when you're ready to make your way back, so make sure you take shoes with you. Flip-flops are better than nothing, but I suggest a pair of water shoes or athletic shoes. (Maybe a pair of Crocs, if you're into that sort of thing.)

Another idea is to find a restaurant where you can hang for a while. Management won't really care how long you stay — as long as you're buying drinks and/or food and your kids don't get too rowdy. Some restaurants cater to vacationers waiting to get into their beach house, making cornhole boards and other activities available. You can also kill some time at one of the large souvenir stores or fishing piers. Dowdy Park in Nags Head is a great place to let the kids run off some energy.

A relatively recent addition to the Outer Banks area is H2OBX Waterpark. Trust me when I say you can't possibly miss it. Its water slides loom tall and colorful on the right-hand side of Rt. 158 in Powells Point, about 12 miles before you reach the Wright Memorial Brothers Bridge that takes you into Kitty Hawk. Its attractions are based on Outer Banks history. There's plenty to keep the family busy, as well as beautiful views, relaxing cabanas, and casual dining options.

Chapter 4 - The Beaches

A whole chapter devoted to the beaches? It's pretty much all the same, isn't it? Sand, water, (hopefully) sun.

Well, yes, all the Outer Banks beaches have those things in common. However, there are beaches that tend to get very crowded during peak season, and there are beaches that are a bit more off the beaten path. Some beaches have lifeguards; some do not. The beach you choose will depend on both your needs and preferences, as well as accessibility.

A general rule is this: Beaches near hotels, whether the hotels are oceanfront or not, are going to be more crowded. No brainer, right? The other locations where you can expect the beach to be more crowded is near public access points. Combine a hotel with a public access point at peak season in the summer, and you can expect to be sharing the beach with a lot of other people.

The further south you go — Nags Head or South Nags Head — the sparser the crowds are. In addition, thanks to sand replenishment, there tends to be a lot more beach in those locations. Frankly, I've encountered beaches in Nags Head that were a little wider than I liked, since it means a very long walk to the water.

Something to keep in mind about the beaches, however, is that, just like the ocean, they change almost constantly. One big storm can render a beach that used to be 100 yards wide little more than a strip of sand big enough for a beach chair. Storms also carve deep cliffs — or shelves, as I call them — into the beach, which can make reaching the water's edge more challenging.

> *And that slow, crooked, seemingly aimless path of our lives at the beach may just be getting us closer and closer to our best selves.* — Sandy Gingras, How to Live at the Beach

Public beach access

Along the beach road between Kitty Hawk and Nags Head, you'll find public access areas. Some of these areas are just a path from the road over the dune to the beach. Others have parking lots, bath houses, wooden walkways, and other handy features, such as handicap parking and beach access, and even pet waste bags. I've listed below some of the areas where you'll find bathrooms or porta-potties, showers, and handicap access.

Kitty Hawk, MP 4, Kitty Hawk Bathhouse: Large Parking Lot, Handicap Parking, Handicap Beach Access, Bath House, Showers and Bathrooms, Lifeguard, Sand Access, Pet Waste Bags.

Kill Devil Hills, MP 6, Hayman Boulevard: Ample Paved Parking (Across Street), Handicap Parking (Across Street),

Outdoor Showers, Lifeguard, Sand Access, Pet Waste Bags, Porta Potty.

Kill Devil Hills, MP 6.5: Paved Parking, Lifeguard, Sand Access, Pet Waste Bags.

Kill Devil Hills, MP 7, 3rd Street: No Parking, Outdoor Showers, Lifeguard, Wooden Walkway, Sand Access, Pet Waste Bags.

Kill Devil Hills, MP 7, 2nd Street: Paved Parking, Outdoor Showers, Lifeguard, Sand Access, Pet Waste Bags.

Kill Devil Hills, MP 7.5, 1st Street: Paved Parking, Outdoor Showers, Lifeguard, Dune Deck, Sand Access, Pet Waste Bags.

Kill Devil Hills, MP 8, Asheville Drive: Paved Parking, Handicap Parking, Outdoor Showers, Porta-potty, Lifeguard, Wooden Walkway, Sand Access, Pet Waste Bags.

Kill Devil Hills, MP 8, Prospect Avenue: Paved Parking, Handicap Parking, Outdoor Showers, Wooden Walkway, Pet Waste Bags.

Kill Devil Hills, MP 8, Glenmere Avenue: Paved Parking, Handicap Parking, Outdoor Showers, Wooden Walkway, Pet Waste Bags. This access point also features a Little Free Library book-sharing location and a Little Red Mailbox where you will find a journal and a pen to record your thoughts as you arrive at or leave the beach.

Kill Devil Hills, MP 8, Ferris Avenue: Ample Paved Parking, Handicap Parking, Outdoor Showers, Wooden Walkway, Pet Waste Bags.

Kill Devil Hills, MP 8, Raleigh Avenue: Paved Parking, Outdoor Showers, Lifeguard, Wooden Walkway, Sand Access, Porta Potty, Pet Waste Bags.

Kill Devil Hills, MP 8, Carlow Avenue: Plenty of Paved Parking, Handicap Parking, Outdoor Showers, Porta Potty, Lifeguard, Wooden Walkway, Bike Rack, Pet Waste Bags.

Kill Devil Hills, MP 8, Sutton Avenue: Ample Paved Parking, Handicap Parking, Outdoor Showers, Lifeguard, Wooden Walkway, Pet Waste Bags.

Kill Devil Hills, MP 8.5, Ocean Bay Boulevard: Paved Parking, Handicap Parking, Handicap Access/Ramps, Stabilizing Sand Mats, Outdoor Showers, Bath House, Lifeguard, Wooden Walkway, Bike Racks, Pet Waste Bags.

Kill Devil Hills, MP 8.5, Oregon Avenue: Paved Parking, Handicap Parking, Outdoor Showers, Lifeguard, Sand Access.

Kill Devil Hills, MP 9, Clark Street: Paved Parking, Outdoor Showers, Lifeguard, Wooden Walkway, Sand Access, Pet Waste Bags.

Kill Devil Hills, MP 9, Martin Street: Paved Parking, Handicap Parking, Outdoor Showers, Lifeguard, Wooden Walkway, Pet Waste Bags.

Kill Devil Hills, MP 9.5, Atlantic Street: Paved Parking, Handicap Parking, Outdoor Showers, Porta-potty, Lifeguard, Wooden Walkway, Sand Access, Pet Waste Bags.

Kill Devil Hills, MP 10, 8th Street: Paved Parking, Handicap Parking, Stabilizing Beach Mat for Wheelchairs, Outdoor Showers, Lifeguard, Wooden Walkway, Sand Access, Pet Waste Bags.

Kill Devil Hills, MP 10.5, Abalone Street: Paved Parking, Porta-potty, Outdoor Showers, Lifeguard, Wooden Walkway, Pet Waste Bags.

Nags Head, MP 10.5, Baltic Street: Paved Parking (limited additional parking across the street), Handicap Parking, Porta-potty, Outdoor Showers, Wooden Walkway, Pet Waste Bags.

Nags Head, MP 10.5, Barnes Street: Paved Parking, Outdoor Shower, porta-potty, Wooden Walkway, Pet Waste Bags.

Nags Head, MP 11, Blackman Street: Paved Parking (additional parking across the street), Handicap Parking, Porta-potty, Outdoor Shower, Wooden Walkway, Pet Waste Bags.

Nags Head, MP 11.5, Bonnett Street: Paved Parking, Handicap Parking, Stabilizing Beach Mat for Wheelchairs, Bath House, Lifeguard, Sand Access, Wooden Walkway, Pet Waste Bags, Picnic Tables, Volleyball Net.

Nags Head, MP 11.5, Bittern Street: Paved Parking, Outdoor Shower, Wooden Walkway, Pet Waste Bags.

Nags Head, MP 11.5, Bladen Street: Paved Parking, Handicap Parking, Porta-potty, Outdoor Showers, Sand Access, Wooden Walkway, Pet Waste Bags.

Nags Head, MP 12, Curlew Street: Paved Parking, Handicap Parking, Porta-potty, Outdoor Shower, Sand Access, Wooden Walkway, Pet Waste Bags.

Nags Head, MP 12, Hollowell Street: Paved Parking, Outdoor Shower, Lifeguard, Wooden Walkway, Pet Waste Bags.

Nags Head, MP 14, Enterprise Street: Paved Parking, Handicap Parking, Porta-potty, Outdoor Shower, Lifeguard, Sand Access, Wooden Walkway, Pet Waste Bags.

Nags Head, MP 14, Loggerhead Street: Paved Parking, Outdoor Shower, Wooden Walkway, Pet Waste Bags.

Nags Head, MP 14.5, Epstein Street: Paved Parking (Additional parking across the street), Handicapped Parking, Bath House, Outdoor Shower, Lifeguard, Wooden Walkway, Pet Waste Bags.

Nags Head, MP 15, Forrest Street: Paved Parking, Handicap Parking, Porta-potty, Outdoor Showers, Lifeguard, Wooden Walkway, Pet Waste Bags.

Nags Head, MP 16, Glidden Street: Paved Parking, Handicap Parking, Outdoor Shower, Wooden Walkway, Pet Waste Bags.

Nags Head, MP 16 to 16.5, between Gray Eagle and Gulfstream Street: Jennette's Pier is at this location and offers beach access, an aquarium, gift shop, snacks, and fishing, as well as paved parking, Handicap Parking, Stabilizing Beach Mat for Wheelchairs, Bath House, Outdoor Showers, Lifeguard, Wooden Walkway, Sand Access, Pet Waste Bags, Porta-potty.

Nags Head, MP 17.5, Hargrove Street: Paved Parking, Handicap Parking, Bath House, Outdoor Showers, Lifeguard, Sand Access, Wooden Walkway, Stabilizing Mat, Pet Waste Bags.

Nags Head, MP 18.5, Indigo Street: Paved Parking, Handicap Parking, Porta-potty, Outdoor Showers, Lifeguard, Bike Rack, Wooden Walkway, Pet Waste Bags.

Nags Head, MP 19, June Street: Paved Parking, Handicap Parking, Porta-potty, Outdoor Shower, Wooden Walkway, Pet Waste Bags.

Nags Head, MP 19.5, Juncos Street: Paved Parking, Handicap Parking, Porta-potty, Outdoor Shower, Lifeguard, Sand Access, Wooden Walkway, Beach Driving Access (seasonal w/ permit), Pet Waste Bags.

Nags Head, MP 26, Coquina Beach: Large Parking Lot, Handicap Parking, Lifeguard, Bath House, Changing Rooms, Outdoor Showers, Water Bottle Filling Station, Wooden Walkway/Dune Deck, Bike Rack, Pet Waste Bags, Entrance to ORV Ramp 2.

Insider Tip: *Do not* **park at Avalon Pier, MP 6. Parking there is by permit only. Nothing ruins a great day on the beach like discovering your car has been towed.**

Beach Access for Those with Mobility Issues

If you're traveling with someone who has mobility issues, look into renting a beach wheelchair. They're designed with large front tires for navigating the sand, and smaller tires in the back to make it easy to steer.

Also, consult the list of public beach access points above for locations that are handicap accessible.

Rental companies for beach wheelchairs:

Ocean Atlantic Rentals - (252) 261-7368

Just For The Beach Rentals - (866) OBX-RENT

Insider Tip: There is a fully handicap accessible beach access point in Kill Devil Hills at Ocean Bay Boulevard.

There are six fixed mats and six rollout mats that allow wheelchair entry onto the beach.

Beaches off the beaten path

Driving south on Rt. 12, past Nags Head, you will reach the Cape Hatteras National Seashore. No hotels or restaurants here. Just beach. Continuing south until you reach the Basnight Bridge — formerly known as the Bonner Bridge — you'll see the Oregon Inlet Marina on your right. To the left is an entrance to the beach known as Ramp 4. When you come to the Outer Banks and you want to find me, this is most likely where I'll be.

Ramp 4 leads to a beach that is accessible only by four-wheel-drive vehicle — or on foot. Driving on the beach requires an off-road vehicle (ORV) permit. If you're only in the OBX for a week, you can purchase a 10-day permit for $50. If you are a frequent visitor, an annual permit is $120 and is valid for one year from the date issued. For information on obtaining a permit, call (252) 475-9054.

Driving on the beach is sometimes restricted due to nesting by protected birds and sea turtles. The National Park Service has an online interactive map you can consult before planning your day on the beach.

Insider tip: Consult a tide chart before you park your vehicle. (You can pick one up at any bait and tackle shop.) If you arrive near low tide, you will want to leave several feet between your vehicle and the water. Remember that the water can be unpredictable, so keep an eye on it. Even if you've left plenty of room, a rogue wave can soak you and everything near you in a matter of seconds.

No four-wheel-drive vehicle? No worries. You can rent one! Outer Banks Jeep Rentals and Enterprise Rent-A-Car, both in Kill Devil Hills, have two-door and four-door

Jeeps available for rent, beach ready and complete with an ORV permit.

Insider tip: Lower your tire pressure before plowing into the sand. If you don't, you can be sure there will be photos posted of you and your stranded vehicle on Facebook. You don't want to end up as part of the gallery on Oregon Inlet Idiots. I recommend a maximum tire pressure of 15 psi, so be sure to bring along a tire gauge. When you leave the beach, you can go right across the street to the marina, where there is an air hose available to the public. (They do ask for donations, make sure to bring along a dollar or two.)

Don't want to buy a permit or rent a four-wheel-drive vehicle? You can still enjoy the uncluttered beaches of the National Seashore. Coquina Beach, about 8 miles south of Nags Head, has a large parking lot and walkways to the beach. There's also a bathhouse and outside showers. (Warning: The water is cold!)

Insider tip: Keep in mind that there are no bathrooms, porta-potties or other modern conveniences on the beach. It's just sand and water. If you need a bathroom, you will have to either walk back to the bathhouse or get back in your vehicle and drive across to the marina.

In addition to the Cape Hatteras National Seashore, driving is permitted in Kill Devil Hills and Nags Head during the off-season, from October 31 through April 30th.

Car Washes

After you've been driving on the beach, you're going to want to get your vehicle washed as soon as possible. If you're renting a house, you may have access to a hose so you can wash your vehicle by hand. It's very important to thoroughly spray off the undercarriage of your car or truck.

There are also two automatic car washes located on Croatan Highway (the bypass). One is at 4011 North Croatan Highway in Kitty Hawk, and the other is at 1814 North Croatan Highway in Kill Devil Hills.

Beach Safety

Sand Safety

Yes, the sand can be dangerous. First of all, in the summer the sand gets hot. Very hot. Like temperature of the sun hot. Do not go out onto the beach without some type of shoes. You may not need them early in the day, but by late morning and early afternoon, you can actually burn the bottom of your feet to the point where they will blister. Also keep in mind that the hot sand can also burn your dog's paws. Best to let your furry family member chill at your beach house during the hottest part of the day.

In addition, digging tunnels or deep holes in the sand can be deadly if the sand caves in and traps someone inside. Rescue can be difficult in sand collapse situations, since the sand will flow back into the hole and can bury a person even as rescuers work to save them.

Another thing to be aware of is the danger of beach umbrellas. To properly secure an umbrella in the sand, first of all, read the instructions that come with it. It's not enough to just stick it in the sand. Rock it back and forth to bury it deeply enough to stay put. At least one-third of the umbrella post should be buried. Open the umbrella and tilt it *into* the wind. Keep an eye on it throughout the day, since the wind can change direction. Consider purchasing an anchor. It makes umbrella setup easier and safer. Also remember to watch out for *other people's* umbrellas!

Swimming

The safest place to swim is in locations where lifeguards are on duty. It's also important to recognize your own limitations. If you can't swim, stay out of the water. Water conditions can change quickly, and you need to have the skills to adapt to the situation you find yourself in. If you're planning an Outer Banks vacation, I strongly encourage you to enroll your children in swimming classes. Always supervise your children closely, even if they're just playing in the sand at the water's edge.

Don't swim alone. Always take along a friend or family member who can call for help if needed. Do not go swimming after you've been drinking. Don't make the mistake of thinking that a blow-up float or boogie board is a lifesaving device. If the water is not shallow enough for you to stand, these devices will not save your life if you get in trouble. They can deflate or be washed away in the surf.

Diving

Unless you are diving with a certified dive instructor who knows where it's safe to do so, just don't. Particularly in the ocean, the conditions change daily. What was deep water yesterday may very well have a hill of sand built up today. Most hotel pools do not allow diving. I have, sadly, known individuals whose lives were changed forever because they misjudged the depth of the water.

Rip Currents

It's critical that you educate yourself and your children about rip currents. A rip current is a strong, localized current. It is relatively narrow and moves directly away from the shore, cutting through the waves. Often you can spot them from the beach. They resemble a river moving away from the shoreline, straight out into the ocean. You may notice a break in the wave pattern and the surface of the water may look foamy. You may also notice a difference in the color of the water in the rip current. For swimmers, knowing how to escape a rip current can quite literally be a matter of life or death.

Swimmers caught in a rip current may find themselves being carried out to sea. The natural inclination is to try to swim back toward shore. However, that's not a fight you will win. You're likely to become exhausted and swimmers caught in a rip current have been known to drown even in shallow water. If you find yourself caught in a rip, it may be difficult to think clearly at that moment, but by arming yourself ahead of time with an understanding of how a rip current works, you have a better chance to escape.

The best thing to do if you become caught in a rip current is to, first, remain calm if you can, and swim parallel to the shore. A rip current is narrow. So, by swimming to either side, you will escape. Another thing to keep in mind is that a rip current does not extend very far out to sea, so there is a limit to how far you could be carried.

The most important thing is to not let yourself become exhausted by attempting to fight the rip current. Swimmers who no longer have the energy to keep themselves afloat are most in danger of drowning.

During peak season, from Memorial Day through Labor Day, the beaches from Kitty Hawk to Nags Head usually have lifeguards stationed every few blocks, with roving patrols continuing through the middle of October. However, at beaches along the Cape Hatteras National Seashore, there are no lifeguards. Park Rangers patrol regularly; however, you are pretty much on your own for beach safety in these locations.

Warning Flags

Sometimes you may notice flags flying at the beach. Don't ignore them. They represent important safety warnings. A yellow flag indicates strong currents; swimmers should use caution. A red flag indicates that swimming is not allowed due to strong currents or rough surf conditions. If you hear someone say, "The red flags are up today," pay attention, even if you don't see the flag.

Sunscreen

Sunscreen is an absolutely essential part of your beach kit. The sun in the summer months, and even as early as April or as late as October, is very strong. **Do not wait** to put on sunscreen. Apply it *before* you head out to the beach, reapply every couple of hours, and help others with you remember to use sunscreen early and often. Don't forget your lips. Make sure you bring along lip balm that contains sunscreen, at least 15 SPF. Also don't forget your ears! If your hair is thinning (or gone), always wear a hat.

Bring a First-Aid Kit

Even if you're on a lifeguarded beach, it's always a good idea to bring along a first aid kit, and it's essential if you're on one of the beaches where lifeguards are not present. Whether it's a minor cut or scrape, or a bug bite, it's important to clean and treat the injury right away. A good camping first aid kit will contain just about anything you need to treat a minor injury, but when in doubt, call 911 right away.

Insider Tip: It's a good idea to pack bug repellant in your beach kit. Often the sea breeze is enough to keep the bugs away, but it's hard to predict when you may encounter biting flies, bees, or other annoying insects, so it's best to be prepared.

Beach Ordinances

Fires

Fires of any kind, including grills, are not allowed on the beach in the Towns of Kitty Hawk, Kill Devil Hills, and Nags Head. Fires are allowed on the National Park beaches, and a permit is not required.

Leaving items on the beach

Do not leave items on the beach overnight. They can easily cause injury to people walking on the beach after dark and could impede hatching turtles from making their way to the water.

Digging Holes

While there are no ordinances against digging holes on the beach, there are rules about filling them in before you leave. They can be surprisingly dangerous. The sand can be heavy and unstable, and rescue attempts after a collapse can be difficult. Worried about sharks? Consider this: There are more beach fatalities each year as a result of collapsing sand holes than there are from shark attacks. My recommendation is that you do not dig a hole, or allow your children to dig a hole, that is deeper than knee height, and always fill it in before you leave. People strolling the beach after dark may not see it and could be seriously injured by stepping or falling into it.

Local Wildlife

On the Outer Banks, we take our wildlife very seriously. They are part of what makes the area so enchanting.

In general, leave the animals alone. If you come across an animal that you believe is injured or in stress, **do not** handle it. There is a high risk for rabies in many wild animals, including bats, raccoons, coyotes, skunks, deer, bears, and turkeys. In addition, it is ***illegal*** to keep wild animals in North Carolina without a permit.

If you come across an injured deer or black bear, contact the NC Wildlife Helpline at 866-318-2401 or the Wildlife Enforcement Division at 800-662-7137.

Nesting sea turtles are particularly important. If you find a dead or injured sea turtle, a stranded turtle, or a turtle nest, notify the Network for Endangered Sea Turtles (NEST) immediately at (252) 441-8622.

Do not allow your children or pets to interact with wildlife. Remember, this is their home. You are a visitor. This includes sea animals that may wash up onshore.

Types of wildlife

Crabs

Blue Crabs

Blue crabs are plentiful in the Outer Banks. You'll find them on the menu of any restaurant that serves fresh local seafood. You're not likely to find one on the beach, but you may want to try your hand at crabbing. For serious crabbing — perhaps enough for dinner one night — check out Chapter 5 for information on crabbing and shrimping charters, or if you want to catch a few just for fun, take a look at Chapter 6.

Ghost Crabs

Atlantic ghost crabs are plentiful in the Outer Banks and are similar to a fiddler crab. They get their name from the fact that they are exactly the same color as the sand, and are almost impossible to spot until they move. During the day, you can spot little ones as they dart in and out of their holes, but they can grow to as large as 2 inches across.

The larger ones tend to come out in the evening to feast on coquina clams or sand crabs. They have long legs and eyes on stalks that can rotate 360 degrees. Don't be surprised if you find a ghost crab or two in the pool of your rental house. Just fish them out and send them on their way.

Horseshoe Crabs

Some people refer to horseshoe crabs as living fossils. They've been around for 350 million years. In truth, they're not really crabs at all. They're more closely related to spiders. Particularly in the spring, which is the horseshoe crab's spawning season, it's not unusual to find them on the beach. Even more common are horseshoe crab egg cases, which are rectangular in shape and black, making them easy to spot.

Sand Crabs

If you visit the Outer Banks in the summer months, it's almost guaranteed that you will see sand crabs, also known as sand fleas. You'll notice them after a wave comes in. As the tide recedes, you'll see them bury themselves back into the sand. They can be anywhere from 1/8th of an inch to 2 inches long and are light gray or slightly pink.

Birds

Seagulls

The laughing gulls are impossible to miss, as their distinctive call gives them their name. They grow to between 14 and 16 inches long, with a wingspan of 39 to 43 inches. They have gray wings and a long red beak. An adult herring gull is 22 to 26 inches long with a wingspan of 54 to 57 inches. They have a yellow beak, slate gray back and wings, and black wing tips spotted with white. At 11 to 15 inches long, the Bonaparte's gull is among the smallest. It's mostly white, with gray on top. During breeding season, which begins in mid-June, they acquire a darker gray hood. Other types of gulls you may see are great black-backed gulls and ring billed gulls.

Terns

The gull-billed tern is also a commonly seen shore bird and looks similar to a seagull. It's about 13 to 17 inches in length and has a wingspan of 30 to 36 inches. It's gray on top and white underneath, with a black cap, black beak, and black legs.

Sandpipers

You will no doubt see these small wading birds at the edge of the surf. There are several types of sandpipers native to the Outer Banks, including the sanderling and purple sandpiper.

Pelicans

One of my favorite birds is the brown pelican. You can see them flying alone over the water or in large squadrons, sometimes in a V-shape or in a line. Watch them as they dive beak-first into the water for fish.

Blue Heron

The magnificent great blue heron stands between 42 and 52 inches tall. I've been fortunate enough to see a couple of them in my own back yard from time to time. You are likely to spot one at just about any time of year in the Outer Banks in areas where there are trees around the water. You may also see the little blue heron, which stands about two feet tall and inhabits saltwater areas.

Egret

The great egret, which is a protected species, can grow to 38 inches tall and often lives nearby its smaller cousin, the snowy egret, which stands about 24 inches tall. They live in shallow wetlands and dine on fish and insects. The great egret also eats frogs and crayfish.

Dolphins

There's a very good chance that you'll spot some dolphins on your trip to the Outer Banks. They are easiest to notice when the water is relatively calm. You'll see them jumping and playing as they move up and down the coast. They can also be spotted in the sound.

Wild Horses

The wild horses of the Outer Banks are believed to be descendants of Spanish horses that found their way to the shore hundreds of years ago after being shipwrecked. The best place to see them is in Corolla, but you may also spot them in Ocracoke and other locations. They are protected by law, and if you interact with them, you will be cited. Admire them from a distance.

Sea Turtles

There are five different types of sea turtles that nest in the Outer Banks. They tend to nest in mounds near the dunes. It's critical that you not disturb the nests. If you find one, call the Network for Endangered Sea Turtles (NEST) immediately at (252) 441-8622.

Wild Boars

You're not likely to see one of these in town or on the beach, but if you're exploring some of the less developed parts of Corolla, you may come across one. They are big, with long tusks and a mean streak, so keep your distance.

Wild Hares

If you're in Roanoke Island around twilight, you may see quite a few of these guys. They are much larger than rabbits, with long ears and long back legs.

Black Bears

Don't be surprised if you see a black bear standing by the side of the road. They are not known to be aggressive, but don't take chances. Leave them alone and do not feed them.

Red Wolves

Red wolves were once believed to be almost extinct, but they have recently made a comeback. You are most likely to spot one near the Alligator River National Wildlife Refuge, and you may even hear them singing at night.

Deer

Deer are very commonly seen in the wooded areas of the Outer Banks, especially in Nags Head, where herds of deer can often be spotted around sunset. If you're out and about around dawn or dusk, keep a lookout for their shining eyes in the brush.

Chapter 5 - Totally OBX Things to Do

Wright Brothers National Memorial

Located in the heart of Kill Devil Hills, the Wright Brothers National Memorial is impossible to miss as you travel south on the bypass (Rt. 158). It's on the exact location where the Wright Brothers achieved their dream of flight. Operated by the National Park Service, you can walk the actual flight line that the Wright Brothers took on their first flights and see exactly how far they were able to fly on each of their first experimental flights. Peek inside reconstructed 1903 camp buildings where the brothers stayed, and walk up the hill to the 60-foot granite monument that commemorates the historic achievements at the site. At the recently remodeled National Historic Landmark Visitors Center, you can view full-scale replicas of the Wright Brothers flyers, and next door at the Centennial of Flight Museum, you can walk through all new exhibits that trace the history of flight from the early 1900s through NASA space flight.

Location: 1000 North Croatan Highway (Bypass), Kill Devil Hills

Insider Tip: The best deal on the entrance fee is to pay per vehicle, rather than per person. The exception to this rule is for a couple with children all under 16,

since everybody under 16 gets in for free. Even better, there are typically several days each year when everyone can get in for free:

Martin Luther King Jr. Day
First Day of National Park Week/National Junior Ranger Day
August 25 – National Park Service Birthday
National Public Lands Day
November 11 – Veterans Day
December 17 – 117th anniversary of the Wright brothers' first flight

Climb a Lighthouse

Cape Hatteras Lighthouse

For more than 200 years, the Cape Hatteras Lighthouse has warned sailors away from the treacherous Diamond Shoals. It is one of the most recognizable structures on the east coast and is the tallest lighthouse in the United States. Formerly perched right on the beach on Hatteras Island, storms took their toll over the years, and in order to preserve the historic lighthouse, the decision was made in 1999 to move it about a half-mile inland to its current location. The lighthouse is maintained by the National Park Service and the U.S. Coast Guard maintains the light, which rotates every 7 seconds and can be seen from 20 miles out to sea.

Insider Tip: If you're physically up to it, climbing the Cape Hatteras Lighthouse is a must. Just understand what you're getting into before you try it. There are height and weight restrictions: You must be at least 42" tall and weigh no more than 260 lbs. There is a total of 257 steps from ground to balcony, with landings after every 31 steps. Only one person at a time is allowed to be on a flight of stairs. There is no elevator and no air conditioning. Climbing the Cape

Hatteras Lighthouse is equivalent to climbing a 12-story building.

If you're good with all that, definitely don't miss it. When you reach the top, you'll be able to enjoy views from the tallest brick lighthouse in America. The lighthouse opens for climbing on the third Friday of April and is open daily through Columbus Day, 9:00 a.m. to 4:30 p.m. There is a small fee (at the time of publication, $8 for adults, $4 for senior citizens and children) and tickets can only be purchased on-site on the day of your climb. Full moon tours are also offered.

The National Park Service occasionally offers fee-free days. Opening day, the first day of the year the lighthouse is open for climbing, is typically the third Friday of April and is a fee-free day. The lighthouse is also open for fee-free climbing for one day during the OBXmas celebration that runs from Thanksgiving through January 6th. Check the National Park Service website for exact date and hours.

Bodie Island Lighthouse

You may also want to consider visiting Bodie Island Lighthouse. If you're staying in Kitty Hawk, Kill Devil Hills, or Nags Head, it's a much shorter drive. Located between Nags Head and Oregon Inlet, the Bodie Island Lighthouse stands 150 feet tall and is open for climbing from late April to early October. Tickets are $10 for adults and $5 for senior citizens and children under 11.

The Lost Colony

Truly an experience for all ages, *The Lost Colony* is the longest running outdoor symphonic drama in America and is an Outer Banks tradition. Based on historic fact, the play tells the story of Roanoke Island, site of the first English settlement in The New World and birthplace of the first English child, Virginia Dare. *The Lost Colony* has been in production since 1937 on the grounds of the Fort Raleigh National Historic Site in Manteo.

The late Andy Griffith performed in *The Lost Colony* during the late 1940s and early 1950s, beginning in the role of a soldier and eventually playing the role of Sir Walter Raleigh. Griffith lived in Manteo until his death in 2012. His television series, *Matlock*, filmed two episodes in the town.

The show is performed on a stage that puts you at the center of the action. The theater was built by President Franklin D. Roosevelt's Works Progress Administration (WPA). More than 4 million tickets have been sold since the play first opened in 1937. Performances of *The Lost Colony* begin on Memorial Day weekend and run through the third week of August. Backstage tours are available prior to the start of the show. The show starts at 7:45 p.m. and runs for 2 hours, with a 15-minute intermission, ending at 10:00 p.m. Purchasing a VIP package provides you with a backstage tour, a souvenir book for adults, a souvenir coin for children, a collectible VIP lanyard, plus you'll have the best seats and early seating.

Location: 1409 National Park Dr, Manteo

Roanoke Island Festival Park

Roanoke Island Festival Park is a 25-acre historic site where you can experience what life was like for the first settlers in the New World, a generation before the Jamestown settlers arrived. Costumed guides show you how the settlers lived, worked, and played in 1585. At the Adventure Museum and American Indian Town, you'll find hands-on interactive exhibits. You can board the Elizabeth II, a replica of the ship that brought the Roanoke Island settlers to America. You'll find sailors in 16th century costumes setting sails and swabbing the decks, and you can even pitch in to help out if you want.

You'll also find the Roanoke Island Freedmen's Colony, which is recognized as a National Underground Railroad to Freedom historic site. It marks a permanent colony that was established on Roanoke Island in the 1860s by former slaves.

Elizabethan Gardens

Also located on Roanoke Island is the Elizabethan Gardens. The idea of creating an authentic garden like the colonists of Roanoke Island might have grown was conceived in the early 1950s. The gardens officially opened in August of 1960 to commemorate the 373rd anniversary of the birth of Virginia Dare. Built on 10 acres of indigenous growth adjacent to The Lost Colony's Waterside Theater and Fort Raleigh National Historic Park, the gardens are open seven days a week (with the exception of certain holidays). You can even bring your dog along!

Location: 1411 National Park Drive, Manteo, (252) 473-3234

Wild Horse Tours

There are few things more "totally OBX" than seeing the wild horses that inhabit the Outer Banks. If you have a four-wheel-drive vehicle, you can see them on your own (more about that in Chapter 6), but a guided tour can be a great way to learn about the history of the horses and the ecology of their environment.

Wild Horse Adventure Tours, 610 Currituck Clubhouse Drive, Corolla, (252) 489-2020

Corolla Wild Horse Tours, 1210 Ocean Trail, Corolla, (252) 207-0511

Back Beach Wild Horse Tours, 817-B Ocean Trail, Corolla, (252) 453-6141

Back Country Safari Tours, 1159 Austin Street, Corolla, (252) 453-0877

Corolla Outback Adventures, 1150 Ocean Trail, Corolla (252) 453-4484

Insider Tip: As you're driving around the Outer Banks, you may spot some of the life-size fiberglass horses that were originally part of a public art exhibit called the Winged Horse Extravaganza that took place from 2002 to 2004. About a third of the horses were sold in an auction to raise money for the Corolla Wild Horse Fund and Monument to a Century of Flight. Several of the horses, however, can still be seen in front of restaurants, businesses, and hotels.

First Flight Adventure Park

Located at MP 15.5 in Nags Head, First Flight Adventure Park (FFAP) is a family fun adventure with obstacle courses and zip lines. FFAP is shaped to resemble the outer bands of a hurricane extending outward from the central tower, which represents the eye of the storm. Obstacles are designed around a maritime theme, with ropes, cables, barrels, and a hammock. Navigate the obstacles, then zip line back to the center. Guides ensure that climbers stay safe, and all climbers are attached to a safety harness. Call ahead to make reservations. Tickets are for 2-hour climbs, and no one under the age of 6 is permitted. Children over the age of 6 are allowed to climb by themselves if they are over 5 feet tall. Otherwise, they need to be accompanied by an adult. If an adult is not available, you can rent a "buddy" to accompany one or two children.

See the Outer Banks from the Air

Air travel began in the Outer Banks, so a tour of the islands from the air is the perfect activity. You'll experience a unique view of the barrier islands and have the opportunity to see dolphins, sea turtles, and shipwrecks. See the lighthouses from a whole new perspective!

Airplane Tours

Barrier Island Aviation - Open-cockpit biplane rides, Cessna rides, and charters.

Location: 407 Airport Road, Manteo, (252) 473-4247

OBX Airplanes - You may see banner planes flying at the beach, or maybe a billboard on your way to the OBX, advertising $15 rides all day. This is where you will find that deal. Keep in mind that the ride is 5 minutes long, so if you're looking for a bit more time in the air, it will cost you more than $15. They offer deals for booking the entire plane, with room for up to 3 passengers, and some packages even allow you to decide whether you want to fly north or south. They also offer sunrise and sunset tours.

Location: 410 Airport Road, Manteo, (252) 489-8165

OBX Air Tour Adventures - This company offers tours in a biplane or a World War II North American AT-6 named Sweet Sophia. They also offer helicopter tours, aerobatic biplane tours, and custom airplane tours for extended time in the air.

Location: 410 Airport Road, Manteo (252) 475-4354

Hang Gliding

Hang gliding, which dates back to the 19th century and is also known as paragliding, involves piloting a light, non-motorized aircraft called a hang glider. The hang glider is constructed of aluminum and strong cloth. It's similar to parasailing (see below) but does not involve the water.

Jockey's Ridge, with the height of the dunes and the strong winds, is the perfect "jumping off point" for taking to the air in a hang glider — and by far the most popular spot for hang gliding. Most flights are 30 to 100 yards long, 5 to 15 feet in the air. Or try tandem hang gliding, where you and your instructor will be towed by an ultralight aircraft to an altitude of more than 2,000 feet. Once released from the aircraft, you will soar like a bird over the Outer Banks.

Kitty Hawk Kites - With multiple locations and boasting that they offer the largest hang-gliding school in the world, Kitty Hawk Kites offers hang gliding for anyone who wants to learn how to fly. From preschoolers to senior citizens, they provide beginner, intermediate, and advanced instruction, as well as tandem instruction for those with physical challenges.

Parasailing

For an amazing bird's-eye view of the Outer Banks, try parasailing. You'll be attached to a canopy, similar to a parachute, and towed by a boat for a fun ride. It's a fun and safe activity for all ages. Little instruction is required. You can fly single, double, or triple, based on weight. Maximum height is 399 feet.

Causeway Watersports - Choose a 500- or 800-foot line or just go out on the boat to observe. Parasail photo packages with up to 60 photos available.

Location: 7649 South Virginia Dare Trail, Nags Head, (252) 441-8875

Kitty Hawk Watersports - Choose from a 400-, 600-, or 800-foot line. Picture package available.

Location: 6920 S Croatan Highway, Nags Head, (252) 441-2756

Kitty Hawk Kites - The crew at Kitty Hawk Kites has over 30 years of experience and offers your choice of Deluxe (400 feet of line), Extreme (600 feet of line), or Ultimate (800 feet of line) parasailing experiences, or you can go as an observer.

Location: 307 Queen Elizabeth Avenue, Manteo, (252) 473-2357

Nags Head Watersports - Offers parasailing from a custom-designed canopy wing.

Location: 7612 South Virginia Dare Trail, Nags Head, (252) 255-5007

Fishing

The first thing you need to know about fishing in the Outer Banks is that, in most cases, you need a license. Children under 16 are exempt, and you don't need a license if you go out on a charter fishing boat or fish from a pier. But if you're surf fishing or fishing from your own boat, you need a license. You can purchase one online from the North Carolina Wildlife Resources Commission. Call 888-248-6834 for more information. Licenses are also available at many tackle shops.

The second thing you may want is a daily fishing report. Most of the local radio stations provide fishing reports. TW's Bait & Tackle provides a daily online fishing report.

Thirdly, you should know that there are some restrictions on the size and number of certain types of fish. These rules can change from time to time, so it's a good idea to check the North Carolina Environmental Quality website for current limits. Ignorance of the law is not an excuse, and if you're stopped with sizes or numbers of fish that violate the restrictions, you will be fined.

Types of fishing

I am no expert on fishing, but I've spent enough time on the Outer Banks to know that there are a variety of different types of fishing: surf, sound, pier, bridge, or offshore. The equipment you'll need varies depending on where you're fishing, and a tackle shop will be able to advise you on what you need. Bluefish, striped bass, and trout are among the most common fish you're likely to catch, but there's quite a few other types of fish that are common to the area, as well. For the "big ones" — tuna, mahi-mahi, marlin, wahoo — look into an offshore charter.

Outer Banks Fishing Charters - Choose a half-day to full-day trip. They also offer 2-hour or 4-hour kids adventure trips.

Location: 19 Thicket Lump Drive, Wanchese, (252) 256-2047

Fish On OBX - Half-day ocean charters for up to 6 people.

Location: 205 North Highway, Manteo, (252) 475-3926

Oregon Inlet Fishing Center - The largest charter boat fishing fleet on the east coast, you'll find a full-service marina and 45 boats available for charter.

Location: 8770 Oregon Inlet Road, Nags Head, (800) 272-5199

Crabbing & Shrimping

For a fun family activity and the opportunity to bring back the very freshest seafood, book a crabbing and shrimping charter. It's a great adventure for all ages.

OBX Crabbing and Shrimping Charters, Wanchese, (252) 423-0421

Grandpa's Charters, Wanchese, (252) 305-8862

Outer Banks Crabbing and Shrimping Charters, Wanchese, (252) 423-0421

NC Crabbing & Shrimping, Manteo, (252) 216-9030

Ghost Tours

OBX Ghost Tours: Take a guided walking tour through downtown Manteo. Enjoy spooky tales of the haunted beaches of the Outer Banks. Release your inner Ghostbuster using a real ghost detector! On the OBX Pirate Walk, you'll hear pirate stories, learn about their history, and even get to take home some booty!

Location:

- Ghost tours meet in front of Downtown Books, 105 Sir Walter Raleigh Street, Manteo, (252) 305-2976

- Pirate tours meet in front of Kitty Hawk Kites, 307 Queen Elizabeth Avenue, Manteo, (252) 305-2976

Visit a Shipwreck

There's believed to be more than 600 shipwrecks off the coast of the Outer Banks. All types of sailing vessels — wooden ships, schooners, battleships, and fishing boats, to name a few— lie at the bottom of the Atlantic in what has been dubbed the Graveyard of the Atlantic. Some of these wrecks are visible, given the right conditions. For some, you'll need to don scuba gear to get a look at them. But there are a handful that can be seen from land.

Lois Joyce - This 100-foot commercial fishing trawler was lost in 1981 as it attempted to navigate Oregon Inlet during a winter storm. The crew was rescued by the Coast Guard, but the ship sank. Head to Oregon Inlet at low tide for a glimpse.

Margaret A. Spencer - The wreckage of this wooden ship can be seen at the shoreline a few miles south of Oregon Inlet.

If you care to venture a bit further south, you can find three more shipwrecks without leaving dry land:

Oriental - Head to Rodanthe to see the wreckage of this Civil War transport steamship that ran aground in 1862. It can be seen just offshore at Pea Island National Wildlife Refuge if the conditions are right.

G.A. Kohler - Stranded on the beach in Salvo in 1933, this four-masted schooner was burned 10 years later to recover her iron fittings. You can see the charred remains at Ramp 27 on the Cape Hatteras National Seashore.

Laura A. Barnes - This four-masted schooner whose home port was in Camden, Maine, set sail from New York, headed to South Carolina, in 1921. She was wrecked on Bodie Island on June 1st, near Coquina Beach. Today you can view the remains at the Graveyard of the Atlantic Museum in Hatteras.

Go to a Brew-Thru

The first Brew-Thru was opened in Nags Head in 1977. Now with five locations in Kitty Hawk, Kill Devil Hills, Nags Head, and Corolla, Brew-Thru is an experience that is both convenient and unique. Your kids will get a kick out of driving right into the store! Just roll down your window and tell the friendly clerk what you want to buy. They carry a large selection of beer, as well as sodas, snacks, and other convenience store items, and you can pick up a tee-shirt, hat, or can koozie.

The Nights in Rodanthe House

If you haven't seen the movie, watch it before or during your trip. Then take a drive south on Route 12 to see the Inn at Rodanthe, where much of the movie was filmed. The house was moved in 2010 to save it from the sea, and it's fairly easy to find. Just turn left on Beacon Road after you enter the Town of Rodanthe, and if you really want the full experience, the house is available for rent. You can also check out the Rodanthe Pier, the location for the filming of the party where the people of the town celebrate after the storm has passed.

Try Some Kill Devil Rum

Outer Banks Distilling is located in downtown Manteo and offers Kill Devil Rum tastings, as well as tours of the distillery. Some believe that Kill Devil Hills took its name from the rum that was being transported in many of the hundreds of ships that sunk in the Graveyard of the Atlantic. It was rum that was manufactured in the Caribbean and said to be strong enough to kill the devil. Legend has it that a horse led along the shore with a lantern around its neck would lure in these ships and they would wreck on the treacherous shoals, and thus, the Town of Nags Head got its name. Barrels of rum plundered from the ships would be hidden behind the hill on which the Wright Brothers Memorial now sits. Thus, the name Kill Devil Hills.

Naturally, the proprietors of the Outer Banks Distillery thought Kill Devil Rum was the perfect name for their spirits. They now sell a variety of rum brewed right on the Outer Banks. Tours are available Tuesday through Saturday. You need a reservation and you must be 21 to take the tour.

Read *Summer Rental* by Mary Kay Andrews

What could be more totally OBX than reading a book set in the Outer Banks while sitting on the beach in the Outer Banks? Be warned, the author took some artistic license. You won't necessarily find all the stores or restaurants she mentions. But one that you *will* find is Bob's Grill. Located in Kill Devil Hills, this unassuming little restaurant is famous for their tagline: *Eat and Get the Hell Out*. The ladies in Andrews' novel are highly amused. And so was Bob's Grill! They have a framed excerpt from the book hanging on their wall.

For other Outer Banks-themed beach reads, check my list in Chapter 9.

Island Farm

Island Farm is located on Roanoke Island. Here the aforementioned Richard Etheridge (Chapter 1) lived as a slave. Island Farm is rich in history and a great way to see what life was like on the Outer Banks in the 19th century. Learn about the impacts of the Civil War on the family who lived here, how they assisted the Wright Brothers in their historical feat, and how they fished in the sound and grew corn for grinding at the windmill. Admission is $8; children under 5 are free. Check their website for a calendar of ongoing events.

Annual Festivals

The Outer Banks is the venue for a number of annual festivals, events spanning a wide range of interests. The exact dates, of course, can vary, so be sure to check the sponsors' websites to find out precisely when an event will take place. Listed below are some of the major events, but be sure to check OuterBanks.org, OuterBanks.com, or

OuterBanksGuides.com to see what's going on while you'll be visiting the Outer Banks.

St. Patrick's Day Parade - Put on the green and find a good spot to view the St. Patrick's Day floats as the parade marches down the Beach Road, starting at MP 11.5. It's a family-friendly way to celebrate the holiday and is the largest St. Patrick's Day parade in North Carolina. Ask at your hotel or vacation rental company about the exact date and starting time.

Outer Banks Wedding Weekend & Expo - If you are planning an Outer Banks wedding, this event should be your first stop. Generally held over the first weekend of March, you'll have the opportunity to visit with over 100 wedding vendors and tour some of the most popular OBX wedding venues. It's a chance to meet with caterers, photographers, rental companies, and lots more. Check the website for exact dates and a list of vendors and venues.

Outer Banks Taste of the Beach - Usually held on the last weekend of March, this event is four days of food, drink, and fun. It's a great opportunity to sample food from different restaurants. Events include wine tastings, cooking classes, brewery tours, tapas crawls, and cookoffs. Check the website for exact dates and list of events.

Flying Pirate Half & First Flight 5K - The Outer Banks Flying Pirate Half-Marathon begins in Kitty Hawk and winds through 13.1 miles of OBX beauty. From the Kitty Hawk Woods Coastal Reserve, along Kitty Hawk Bay and Colington Creek, to the Wright Brothers National Memorial, finishing at the Nags Head Woods Preserve, you'll be rewarded at the finish line with a Pirate Jamboree featuring live music, food, fun, and beer. There's also a 5K and a Fun Run that skirt around the Wright Brothers monument. Typically held on the third Sunday of April.

Location: 5300 The Woods Road, Kitty Hawk, (252) 255-6273

Hang Gliding Spectacular - This is the world's oldest continually running hang gliding meet. Typically held in May, with four full days of events taking place at various locations. Check the Kitty Hawk Kites website for details.

Rock the Cape Festival - Beginning on Memorial Day weekend, this festival runs for two full weeks and features live entertainment, watersports, an art show, and more. The festival began in 2012 as a way to celebrate local artists.

4th of July - Obviously, this is an annual event not exclusive to the Outer Banks ... but there's no better place to be to celebrate our country's freedom! You can start your day with a parade in Duck, then move on to Manteo and Roanoke Island Festival Park for small town events and music from military bands. Of course, no 4th of July celebration would be complete without fireworks. There are typically four fireworks displays — Avalon Pier, Nags Head Fishing Pier, Manteo, and Avon Pier. Important: If you want to set off your own fireworks, take note that North Carolina State law allows only what they call "safe and sane" fireworks. This basically means sparklers, fountains, and other pyrotechnics that do not launch into the air. However, in Nags Head and other parts of the Outer Banks, **all fireworks are illegal**. Check with your hotel or vacation rental company to find out the current laws for the town you are visiting.

Insider Tip: Climb to the top of Jockey's Ridge for a spectacular view of the Nags Head and Manteo fireworks displays.

Outer Banks Seafood Festival - Typically held on the third weekend of October, this festival is a seafood lover's dream. Restaurants from all over the Outer Banks serve up some of their best dishes. Pair your favorites with a local wine or frosty brew, enjoy great live entertainment, and shop at dozens of vendors for unique Outer Banks arts and crafts, educational opportunities, as well as a chance to support local charities.

Location: 6800 South Croatan Highway (Bypass MP 16.5), Nags Head, NC 27959

Hangin' With Santa & Kites With Lights - If you visit the Outer Banks during the Thanksgiving weekend, take your kids for free photos with Santa and check out some classic toys in the Kitty Hawk Kites workshop. Don't miss the unique light show on the Saturday after Thanksgiving, featuring 19-to-30-foot kites lit up for the season and the lighting of the Jockey's Ridge State Park solar Christmas tree.

Location: Kitty Hawk Kites, Jockey's Ridge Crossing, Nags Head

Chapter 6 - Budget-friendly activities

Let's face it: A trip to the Outer Banks can be pricey. If you've rented a cottage for the week, you've likely already invested hundreds, if not thousands, depending on how many family members or friends you're splitting the cost with. You're eating in restaurants, paying for admission to attractions, and buying t-shirts, hooded sweatshirts, and coffee cups to commemorate your trip. Heck, even miniature golf can run you $10 per person!

For me, personally, give me a week of good weather and I am perfectly happy to spend every single day soaking up the sun and listening to the crashing waves.

To escape and sit quietly on the beach - that's my idea of paradise. — Emilia Wickstead

But not everyone is like that, and particularly if kids are part of your vacation, there's a good chance you may want to take a break from the beach for a day — or part of a day — and there are plenty of family-friendly attractions to choose from.

So, here's a list of activities you can do for free. Just add some childlike energy and a sense of adventure — and be sure to take lots of pictures!

Jockey's Ridge State Park

Jockey's Ridge is the tallest "living" sand dune on the east coast. Covering 426 acres, the dune sometimes reaches a height of 60 feet. The nearby maritime thicket features a variety of native trees, such as live oaks, red cedar, and bayberry. However, the effects of sand and salt result in the growth of the trees being stunted, so they appear more as shrubs. You may also spot a fox, deer, or raccoon in the thicket. Also, part of the park is the Roanoke Sound Estuary, home to a variety of plant, animal, and bird life. The dune itself is the perfect place to go kite-flying or take some great photographs.

Insider Tip: If you climb the dune in the summer, remember that the sand gets extremely hot. Be sure to wear sturdy shoes, and don't forget the sunscreen!

You may have heard the rumors about the dune at Jockey's Ridge devouring a miniature golf course. It's true, and sometimes you can see the proof. Depending on how the wind has been blowing when you drive by on the bypass, you can see the tops of a castle that once belonged to this ill-fated mini-golf course.

Hatteras/Ocracoke Ferry

Operated by the North Carolina Department of Transportation, the Hatteras/Ocracoke Ferry runs 365 days a year. This free 45-minute ride is a great way to see the Outer Banks from a different perspective. Once you arrive on Ocracoke Island, you can explore the island by car or have a picnic on the beach. There are also two dozen restaurants or so restaurants where you can grab a bite to eat. You can rent a golf cart for a fun way to tool around the island or you can take an island boat tour.

Insider Tip: The ferry used to be a well-kept secret but is now a very popular attraction. It can get quite busy in the summer. To avoid lengthy wait times, it's

best to plan your trip for Monday or Friday, as Tuesdays through Thursdays tend to be the busiest.

While you're in Ocracoke, visit the Ocracoke Lighthouse. It's the oldest operating lighthouse on the North Carolina coast. It was built in 1823 to replace the original 1803 tower after it was destroyed by lightning in 1818.

Wild Horses

You've probably heard about the wild horses of the Outer Banks, sometimes called Banker horses. They are descended from domesticated Spanish horses believed to have been brought to America in the 16th century. Exactly how they came to make the Outer Banks their home is something of a mystery, but it's assumed that they either survived a shipwreck and swam ashore, or were abandoned. At one time, they numbered in the thousands. Now there's only about 100 of them left.

To see them, head north to Corolla. The horses tend to congregate in small herds in the four-wheel-drive areas of the beach, so you'll need a four-wheel-drive vehicle, or you can take a guided tour. (Wild horse tours don't really fit into the "budget-friendly" category, so I've included more information on that in Chapter 5.) You can't get too close, so if you want to take photos, bring along your zoom lens. If you opt for the do-it-yourself trip to see the horses, *drive slowly*. Horses have been killed by people driving too fast on the beach, and that's not a good memory of your vacation.

Insider Tip: Currituck County has established a number of laws regarding human interaction with the horses. First, *do not feed* them. People tend to offer them apples and carrots, but these foods can actually kill the wild horses. Their digestive systems are very sensitive, and they can tolerate only the foods that

grow naturally in their environment, such as seagrass, sea oats, acorns, and persimmons. It is also illegal to pet a wild horse. In fact, it's illegal to be within 50 feet of them. The laws apply to humans, not the horses, so if a horse approaches you, it is up to you to move away from it. *Do not* attempt to entice a horse to get closer — so you can get a better photo, for example. Many of these laws were enacted because horses that become habituated to humans must be removed from the herd for the protection of the other horses. Once a horse is removed from the beach, it is never allowed to return. Keep in mind that local law enforcement vigorously enforces these rules, and you *will* be ticketed if you're caught breaking them. Fines can be as high as $500 for a first offense.

Alligator River National Wildlife Refuge

Just across the Manns Harbor Bridge in Manteo is Alligator River National Wildlife Refuge. With 15 miles of roads, this is a great opportunity to spot black bears, wild turkeys, birds of prey, and maybe even a red wolf. Pick up a map at the kiosk at Creef Cut Wildlife Trail and explore the roads on your own or take a guided tram tour (operating weekly during the summer). The wildlife does not see vehicles as a threat, so stay in the comfort (and safety) of your car and get some great photos.

Monument to a Century of Flight

Visit the Monument to a Century of Flight in Kitty Hawk, next to the Outer Banks Visitors Center. This park is a well-kept secret and consists of 14 stainless steel columns shaped like wings. They range in height from 10 feet to 20 feet, which commemorates the distance of 120 feet that the Wright Brothers achieved with their first flight in December of 1903. The women and men of air flight and space flight are recognized here. It also includes a bronze dome depicting the 7 continents of the globe. The bottom of the dome shows depictions of various aircraft, from blimps and hot air balloons to helicopters, jet planes, and fighter jets. The park is open to the public and there is no admission charge.

Beachcombing

The sea does not reward those who are too anxious, too greedy, or too impatient. One should lie empty, open, choiceless as a beach - waiting for a gift from the sea. — Anne Morrow Lindbergh

I'm going to be honest: Beachcombing can be hit or miss. Some days, you will find more shells that you can collect; other days, there's nothing. If you're having one of those days where it's slim-pickin's, try moving away from the water and closer to the dunes. There's a good chance you'll find some shells there.

Insider Tip: In general, the best time to do your beachcombing is at low tide, particularly early morning low tide. Pick a tide chart at any bait and tackle shop.

If it's a good day and you're finding lots of treasures along the surfline, be sure to look for sea glass. My experience is that sea glass is fairly rare — I've found a total of three pieces in the last five years or so — but I've known of people who got really lucky and found lots of it.

Insider Tip: Sea glass, or beach glass, is glass that has been worn smooth by the ocean, wind, and sand. They have a "frosted" appearance and soft edges. Something as ordinary as a piece of an old soft drink bottle can become a beautiful gem after being transformed by the sea.

If you happen to be vacationing right after a hurricane — hopefully one that has stayed well off the coast — that can be a really great time for beachcombing. I've found conch shells, starfish, and sand dollars following big storms. The winter months also provide a good opportunity for finding beach treasures. Bundle up and head out on a sunny day in February, and chances are good that you'll have the beach to yourself!

Insider Tip: Be sure to bring along a bucket or bag to carry your collection. You'll find mesh bags in the beach shops that are perfect for collecting seashells, and you'll also find beachcombing nets (very much like a butterfly net) that can be fun for scooping up shells right at the surf line, where they often collect in piles but are difficult to grab in your hand as the waves crash in and out.

You may find live bivalves, such as mussels. I don't recommend collecting these. There's no law against it, but if you're thinking you'll steam and eat them, consider this: You don't know how long they've been lying on the beach, baking in the sun. If you collect them and leave them in your bucket or bag, they will quickly turn into a stinky mess. Best to observe them, explain to your kids what they are, and then maybe throw them back into the sea.

Skateboarding

If you or someone in your party is a skateboarder, be sure to bring along a board. The multi-use paths along the Beach Road are available to skateboarders, or you can check out one of the skate parks in Kitty Hawk or Nags Head. Be sure to bring along a helmet and pads. You can't skate without them at these facilities. If you didn't bring a skateboard with you, check my list of surf shops at the end of Chapter 7. Many of them also sell skateboards.

Kitty Hawk Skate Park

Location: 900 W. Kitty Hawk Road, Kitty Hawk (252) 475-5920

Nags Head Skate Park is on the premises of the YMCA and open from 8:00 a.m. to sunset.

Location: 3000 South Croatan Highway (Bypass MP 11), Nags Head (252) 441-5508

Crabbing

I'm not a huge fan of crabs — mixed into a hot dip, they're pretty good — but I know I'm in the minority. This activity is free if you're lucky enough to find a collapsible crab pot or ring net at your rental. Even if you have to buy one, you can pick one up pretty cheap, under $10. Check bait and tackle shops, which are plentiful on the Outer Banks. If you use one of the rectangular crab traps, you'll need a license.

You'll also need some nylon rope and a mesh bait bag in which to place some raw chicken or meat in the net. A wing or a thigh will do. Attach the rope to your net and place the bait bag inside the net. By using a bait bag, you can minimize the chance that your bait will float away, or some sneaky crab will grab it and take off. Tie the bag to the bottom of your net with the attached strings.

Then you just need to find a place to drop your crab net in the water. Venture over to Pamlico, Albemarle, or Pamlico Sound. I've known of people who have good luck dropping their net in the surf, but in general, sound waters are preferable, especially near a bridge or pier. Slowly lower the net into the water — you'll want your net to sit on the floor of the water — tie off the rope, and wait. Plan some other activities for while you're waiting, like fishing or taking pictures. Check your net every 10 minutes or so.

Pull the net up quickly so the water pressure will keep the crabs at the bottom.

If you harvest some crabs that are big enough to eat, take 'em home and cook 'em! Little ones — and any that you don't plan to eat — should be thrown back. Be sure to clean up the area before you leave, and take all your equipment with you. Don't throw any of it into the water, because some of it is not biodegradable.

Visit Jennette's Pier

Jennette's Pier is the oldest fishing pier in the Outer Banks. It was built in 1939, and over the years, hurricanes and storms took their toll. In 2003, shortly after it was acquired by the North Carolina Aquarium Society, the pier was destroyed by Hurricane Isabel. After two years of reconstruction, a reimagined Jennette's Pier opened to the public, featuring educational programs, live animal exhibits, and demonstrations of alternative energy sources, as well as fishing supplies and a snack bar. The fee to walk out on the pier is just $2 for adults and $1 for kids, making this an "almost free" activity, but you may want to reserve a spot in a fishing class or ghost crab hunt, which costs a little more.

Location: Beach Road MP 16

Go Sand Sledding

What's sand sledding, you ask? Well, the Outer Banks doesn't see a lot of snow, so there's not much opportunity for sledding. Never the type to miss out on the fun, OBX locals go sand sledding instead, which doesn't require any equipment beyond a flatten cardboard box. Don't try this on the dunes by the beach, however; they are protected by law and you shouldn't walk or climb on them. Go to Jockey's Ridge for this activity. You can also try out sandboarding, which is similar to snowboarding; however, the sand presents a more challenging environment than snow. You don't need a permit for either of these activities unless your sandboard has bindings.

Bird Watching

Some people plan their entire trip to the Outer Banks just for the purpose of bird watching. There is an official North Carolina Birding Trail that includes several locations on the Outer Banks. Among them are the Elizabethan Gardens, Jockey's Ridge, Bodie Island, and Cape Hatteras National Seashore. The types of birds you can see will depend on your exact location and the time of year.

I personally love the brown pelicans. They fly in V-shaped "squadrons" and it's fun to watch them drop out of the sky, beak pointed straight down, diving for fish. On one day trip to the Cape Hatteras National Seashore, we saw hundreds and hundreds of American black ducks flying by. They seemed to go on forever.

The laughing gull is easiest to recognize, for obvious reasons, and is the type of gull you're most likely to find in the Outer Banks. They are the largest of the gulls, with black heads and black wing tips.

Insider Tip: Though it may be tempting, it's not a good idea to feed the seagulls. You may notice them inching closer when they realize you've broken out the chips or fried chicken. Trust me on this: If you feed them, you will soon be surrounded, and while they won't hurt you, they'll get on your nerves eventually. When my boys were little, they were playing with some multicolored small plastic dinosaur toys at the beach. An orange one got buried in the sand, with only the tip of its tail showing, and a seagull tried to pluck it out of the sand and fly off with it, apparently thinking it was a cheese curl.

With its variety of ecosystems, Jockey's Ridge is a great place for bird watching. In addition to the dune system, Jockey's Ridge includes a maritime forest, wetlands, and the Roanoke Sound. You can see osprey, blue herons, and snowy egrets, among several other varieties of birds.

By some accounts, as many as 175 different bird species have been spotted at the Elizabethan Gardens. In the spring and fall, migrant songbirds are known to make a stop there, and there's plenty of trails to explore among the pines, Magnolia trees, and other hardwood trees.

For a birding location off the beaten path, visit the marsh on Roanoke Island. Swans and American black ducks are among the species that winter in the area, and you may also be able to spot large birds of prey, such as osprey, wading through the marsh.

Pea Island is another great place for bird watching. Established in 1938, its purpose is to be a nesting and wintering habitat for migratory birds, as well as endangered animals such as Loggerhead turtles. It was also intended to provide a place where the public can enjoy the wildlife and wetlands.

Location: 14500 NC Highway 12, Rodanthe, (252) 987-2394

Nags Head Beach Cottage Row

The Nags Head Beach Cottage Row District consists of three dozen homes, most of which began as shacks that were built from wood scavenged from the beach, leftovers from shipwrecks that washed up on shore. The first of these small cottages was built in the early 1800s.

Location: Beach Road MP 12

Biking, Walking, and Jogging

The Outer Banks is a great place for biking, walking, and jogging. A brisk walk along the beach is the perfect way to start your day — or a leisurely stroll if that is more your speed. You'll see walkers, joggers, and bikers on both the Beach Road and the Bypass, where there are dedicated bike lanes and signs encouraging drivers to share the road. Jockey's Ridge and the Wright Brothers Memorial are also great places to walk or jog.

In addition, there are several multi-use trails designed for biking, walking, and running. You can enjoy biking even if you don't bring a bike with you. I've listed below some bike rental companies. You can even have a bike delivered to your vacation rental.

Bike Rental Shops

Kitty Hawk Cycle Company, (252) 261-2060
Just For The Beach Rentals, (866) OBX-RENT
Ocean Atlantic Rentals, (252) 261-7368
OBX Toy Rentals, (252) 715-5141
Outer Banks Bicycle, (252) 480-3399

Kitty Hawk Woods Reserve

Bordering the Currituck Sound, Kitty Hawk Woods Coastal Reserve includes a multi-use path maintained by the Town of Kitty Hawk. The trail winds through maritime forests and you'll have the opportunity to see ancient dunes that stand up to 30 feet tall. With its towering trees and freshwater ponds, you may come across tree frogs, salamanders, turtles, and even snakes. (Not to worry — the snakes are not likely to be interested in you, although you should be aware that some may be venomous.) Migratory birds use the area as a rest stop, and a variety of wildlife and aquatic animals make the reserve their home. It's important to remember not to disturb or feed the wildlife. Admire them from afar. Bring a camera with a zoom lens to capture the beauty of the animals and birds you encounter.

At Sandy Run Park, which is part of Kitty Hawk Woods Coastal Reserve, you'll find a raised wooden walkway, two gazebos, a covered picnic pavillion, grills, a putting green, and a half basketball court. There is also plenty of parking and access to a canoe/kayak canal. Bring your rod and reel to fish the stocked pond from the pier. (Remember, you need a license to fish.)

Kitty Hawk Woods is also home to another park, the David Paul Pruitt Jr. Park. It's a small recreation area with a playground and picnic tables. It also includes a multi-use path for walking, jogging, or biking.

Location: You can access the trail from Birch Lane, West Eckner Street, or Barlow Lane in Kitty Hawk.

Nags Head Woods Preserve

This maritime forest is definitely off the beaten path. Many people don't even know it's there. Situated between dune ridges that shield it from ocean winds, Nags Head Ecological Woods Preserve is home to many types of animals and plant life not typically found on a barrier island. The canopy created by the towering trees, some of them hundreds of years old, is more typically found in the mountains. Dozens of bird species, as well as a variety of reptiles and amphibians, are found in the preserve, along with rare plant and animal species. There are eight miles of hiking trails, as well as bike paths, and the preserve is also a beautiful location for bird watching and photography. The trails wind through forest and dune habitats, as well as swamp and pond areas. The preserve is also home to cemeteries and farm sites that date as far back as the 19th century. The trails are open to the public between 10:00 a.m. and 3:00 p.m. on weekdays. There are some restrictions on bicycling and pets.

Location: 701 West Ocean Acres Drive, Kill Devil Hills, (252) 441-2525

Libraries

For me, there are few things more relaxing than putting my toes in the sand and my nose in a book. You're likely to find a selection of books at your vacation rental. But if not, you can always head to the library.

Little Free Library - There are three Little Free Library locations, one in Kitty Hawk and two in Kill Devil Hills. Stop by and pick up a book or donate one. You don't have to return the book you borrow, but help keep the library stocked for others by contributing.

Art's Place, 4624 North Virginia Dare Trail (Beach Road), Kitty Hawk

Glenmere "Hope" Beach Access, Kill Devil Hills

Ocean Bay Boulevard Beach Access, Kill Devil Hills

Kill Devil Hills Library - Unless you have a Dare County library card, you can't check out books, but they have daily story times for kids, as well as computers and wi-fi access. It's also a great place to browse Outer Banks historical information and maps.

Location: 400 Mustian Street, Kill Devil Hills, (252) 441-4331

Where to view sunrise/sunset

If you're staying in an oceanfront cottage or hotel room, viewing the sunrise is a no-brainer. All you really have to do is get up before the sun does.

At the beach, life is different. Time doesn't move hour to hour but mood to moment. We live by the currents, plan by the tides and follow the sun. – Sandy Gingras, How To Live At the Beach

If, however, you're not staying right on the beach — or you want to get a really amazing photo of the sunrise that's a bit more creative than the sand, the ocean, and the sun, try some of these spots for a great view:

- Kitty Hawk Boat Ramp - Standing on the docks, you can get a beautiful shot of the sunrise or the sunset.

- Bay Drive, Kill Devil Hills - The sunset photo above was taken at a public access point at the end of 3rd Street, looking across Kitty Hawk Bay.

- Roanoke Island Festival Park - There is a path around the perimeter of the park, providing an opportunity to find the perfect shot.

- Bodie Island Lighthouse - Walk out to the end of the boardwalk for a spectacular view.

The sunset on the Outer Banks is usually spectacular no matter where you're located. However, if you want to get a really good view – or a really good photo – without power lines and other structures obstructing your view, you need to be on the sound side of the island. Here's a few places you can get a breathtaking view of the sunset:

- Jockey's Ridge – From the top of Jockey's Ridge, you can enjoy a 360° view of the Outer Banks, and the view of the sunset from this vantage point is amazing.

- Colington Harbour – From the bypass, turn left on Colington Road, just past the Wright Brothers Memorial.

- Pamlico Jack's – At time of publication, Pamlico Jack's was still open, although the property has been sold to the Town of Nags Head to expand their festival grounds. They have a lovely deck where you can dine and enjoy the sunset, and they even post the time of sunset on their sign out front.

- West 3rd Street Public Estuarine Access – The photo above was captured at this location. At the intersection of Bay Drive and 3rd Street, there is a public gazebo that's perfect for watching the sunset.

The Piers

Take a relaxing stroll along one of the Outer Banks' many piers. Most charge only a small fee if you aren't going to be fishing. Here's a list of the piers from Kitty Hawk to Nags Head.

- Kitty Hawk Pier
- Avalon Pier
- Nags Head Fishing Pier
- Jennette's Pier
- Outer Banks Fishing Pier

Chapter 7 - Water Activities

Naturally, when you're in the Outer Banks, you're likely to be primarily interested in water activities. Whether you're a thrill-seeker, looking for some great photo opportunities, or just want a relaxing cruise, there's something for everyone. In this chapter, I list the many water activities available to you on the OBX, and at the end of the chapter you will find a list of companies that offer these and lots of other exciting adventures.

Jet Skiing

Take a tour or you rent a jet ski and chart your own course. In general, the rules require that the person operating the jet ski must have a valid driver's license and there are age restrictions for riders, depending on whether you rent your own jet ski or book a tour.

Kiteboarding

Also known as kitesurfing, kiteboarding is easy to learn but is sure to get your blood pumping. Pilots try to catch the air and spin, flip, or just fly — for distances as far as the length of a football field!

Wakeboarding

Wakeboarding is similar to water skiing, but the idea is for the boat to achieve a speed high enough to create a wake. The wake allows the rider to jump and perform aerial maneuvers. Take a private lesson and ski till you drop!

Tubing

This isn't like white-water tubing that you may have heard about or experienced. Tubing on the Outer Banks is a little more laid back, so just about anyone can participate. The tube is towed by a boat, and you can book a tubing adventure where you and your family or friends (up to 12) can have a tube all to yourselves.

Paddle Boarding

For many people, when they think of paddle boarding, they think of stand-up paddle boarding, but it can also include lying or kneeling on a board. Stand-up paddle boarding is easier than it looks, and it's a great workout!

Surfing

Many people don't think of the east coast when they think of great surfing locations, but the Outer Banks can be a great place to catch some waves. Not only is it perfect for beginners, there are also some spots that are notorious for "epic" waves! If you happen to be vacationing right after a storm, you're likely to find big waves everywhere. Otherwise, the area around the piers are generally a good place to go. Local regulations require surfers to stay at least 100 years away from the pier, but good waves extend beyond that point. Want to learn how to surf? No problem. There are several places in the Outer Banks where you can get surf lessons.

Scuba Diving

One of the coolest things about diving in the Outer Banks is the opportunity to view the remains of one of the many shipwrecks. They don't call it the Graveyard of the Atlantic for nothing! Here are a few of the shipwrecks you could encounter:

The Winks Wreck can be found near MP 2 in Kitty Hawk, about 120 yards offshore. The wreck was named for Winks Store, which was located nearby on the Beach Road. The exact identification of the ship is not known.

The Triangle Wrecks are located near MP 7 in Kill Devil Hills. Both *the Kyzickes* and the *Carl Gerhard* ran aground at the exact same location, two years apart, *The Kyzickes* in 1927 and the *Carl Gerhard* in 1929. The wreckage of the two ships lies in the shape of a triangle (hence the name) between 100 yards and 250 yards offshore.

The Huron sank in November of 1877 as it set sail to Havana. Usually marked by buoys, you can find it about 200 yards off the coast in Nags Head, between MP 11 and 12.

Kayaking

With its variety of water bodies, the Outer Banks is a great place for kayaking. Kayaking gives you the opportunity to enjoy the pristine waterways and natural beauty, maybe even enjoy a breathtaking sunset over the water.

Boat Cruises and Tours

If a quiet cruise on a boat is more your speed, there's plenty to choose from.

Dolphin Tour

Dolphins are plentiful off the Outer Banks. There's a good chance you'll spot from the beach as they frolic and search for a meal. To learn more, take a dolphin cruise. These tours are run by biologists as part of their research, so in addition to it being a fun activity, it's also educational. You can learn how scientists conduct their research and what they've learned about the animals from their monitoring efforts over the years. Passengers also learn about island birdlife, such as ospreys and pelicans. You'll board a covered pontoon boat and set out from Roanoke Sound for a two-hour trip. The dolphins are drawn to the wake of the boat. It's a great opportunity to capture a video, or if your timing is right, snap an action photo. A dolphin cruise is truly the perfect family activity.

Sunset Cruise

There are few things more breathtaking (or romantic) than an Outer Banks sunset, and one of the best ways to experience it is with a sunset cruise in the Roanoke Sound. Bring along a cooler and enjoy drinks and a picnic dinner onboard. (Guys, it's the perfect place for a proposal. Just sayin'.)

Airboat Tours

For a different view of the Outer Banks, an airboat tour could be the perfect adventure for your family. Suitable for all ages, you can take a sunrise or sunset cruise, a historical tour, or an eco-tour.

For just about every type of water adventure you can imagine, check out these companies:

Captain Johnny's Dolphin Tours, (252) 473-1475
- Morning, Afternoon, and Sunset Dolphin Tours

Causeway Watersports, (252) 441-8875

- Jet ski rentals and tours
- Tubing
- Paddle boarding
- Kayak rentals

Coastal Kayak Touring Company, (252) 441-3393
- Paddleboard tours and rentals
- Kayak rentals and tours

Kitty Hawk Kites, (877) FLY-THIS
- Jet ski rentals and tours
- Kiteboarding
- Wakeboarding
- Tubing trips
- Paddle boarding
- Surfing lessons
- Dolphin tours
- Sunset cruises
- Kayak tours

Kitty Hawk Surf Co., (877) FLY-THIS
- Jet ski tours
- Paddle boarding
- Surfing lessons
- Kayaking

Kitty Hawk Watersports, (252) 441-2756
- Jet ski rentals and tours
- Paddleboard rentals and lessons
- Surfboard rentals
- Kayak rentals and tours
- Dolphin tours
- Sailboat rentals and lessons

Nags Head Dolphin Watch, (877) FLY-THIS
- Dolphin Tours

Nags Head Watersports, (252) 255-5007
- Jet ski rentals
- Paddle boarding
- Kayak rentals

Outer Banks Adventures, (757) 871-6402
- Paddleboard rentals and lessons
- Airboat tours

Outer Banks Kayak Adventures, (252) 489-8146
- Kayak rentals and tours

Outer Banks Bicycle, (252) 480-3399
- Kayak rentals
- Paddleboard rentals
- Surfboard rentals

The Pit Surf Shop, (252) 480-3128
- Paddleboard rentals and lessons
- Surfboard rentals and surf lessons
- Skim board rentals

Scammell's Corner Surf Shop & Ice Cream Parlor, (252) 715-1727
- Surfboards sales and rentals
- Surf lessons

Wave Riding Vehicles, (757) 422-0423
- Surfboard sales
- Surf lessons

Outer Banks Boarding Company, (252) 441-1939
- Surfboard sales and rentals
- Paddleboards

Secret Spot Surf Shop, (252) 441-4030
- Surfboard rentals
- Surf lessons

FarmDog Surf School, (252) 255-2233
- Surfboard rentals
- Surf lessons

Chapter 8 - Kid Friendly Activities

Kids love the beach. With their plastic buckets and shovels in tow, maybe a toy dump truck, some plastic dinosaurs, sometimes just a red Solo cup, most kids can entertain themselves for hours with the sand, looking for seashells, and enjoying the wildlife. But every once in a while, you may want to take a break from the beach and find some other activities where kids can be kids, and all of you can make memories. In this section, you'll find some of my best suggestions.

Adventure

First Flight Adventure Park - For ages 6 and up, First Flight Adventure Park is a family fun adventure with obstacle courses and zip lines. It's shaped to resemble the outer bands of a hurricane extending outward from the central tower, the eye of the storm. Obstacles are designed around a maritime theme, with ropes, cables, barrels, and a hammock. Navigate the obstacles, then zip line back to the center. Guides ensure that climbers stay safe, and all climbers are attached to a safety harness. Call ahead to make reservations. Children must be at least 5 feet tall to climb by themselves. Otherwise, they need to be accompanied by an adult. If an adult is not available, you can rent a "buddy" to accompany 1 or 2 children. Location: Bypass MP 15.5

Be a Junior Ranger - For ages 5 to 13, the Cape Hatteras National Seashore Junior Ranger program guides kids through a series of activities to earn their Junior Ranger badge. Stop by any visitor center to pick up a booklet of activities.

Art

OBX Art Studio is a family-oriented do-it-yourself art studio, open year-round. Relax, unwind, and try your hand at creating art using a variety of media — from pottery painting to canvas art.

Location: 2200 North Croatan Highway (Bypass MP 6), Kill Devil Hills, (252) 449-2134

Life on a Sandbar is a unique store offering hair wraps, henna tattoos, and jewelry, but it's also a great place for kids' activities. Make a decorative sand casting or steppingstone. Or create a work of art by casting your child's hands to commemorate her or his first trip to the Outer Banks.

Location: 3933 South Croatan Highway (Bypass MP 12.5), Nags Head, (252) 449-9066

Bowling

Head to the OBX Bowling Center in Nags Head. They offer Open Bowl, Late Night Rock 'N Bowl, plus an arcade and an up-to-date game room. Enjoy all the usual bowling alley fare at the snack bar.

Location: 200 West Satterfield Landing Road (turn left off the Bypass at MP 10), Nags Head, (252) 255-1187

Indoor Trampoline Park

Jumpmasters - This 14,000-square-foot indoor trampoline park is the one-of-a-kind on the Outer Banks. It's a place for all ages and includes lots of fun activities like dodgeball, battle beam, and a ninja warrior course. There's also a climbing wall and a foam pit. There's even a special "toddler time" on Saturday mornings.

Location: 28 U.S. Highway 64, Manteo, (252) 423-3177

Laser Tag

Outer Banks Gearworks - With state-of-the-art laser tag, the Gearworks Family Fun Center is great for all ages. Whether you participate in the game or watch from the observation deck, Gearworks is packed with fun and the perfect thing for a rainy day. You can lose yourself in the game or hang out in the arcade.

Location: 2420 South Croatan Highway (Bypass MP 10.5), Nags Head, (252) 480-8512

Miniature Golf

Mini golf is the perfect family activity. You'll find several miniature golf courses between Kitty Hawk and Nags Head.

Lost Treasure Golf, 1600 North Croatan Highway, Kill Devil Hills. Based on the adventures of the fictional Professor Duffer A. Hacker from the University of Chicago, the old mining train he discovered on his hunt for the Lost Colony will take you to the first holes of the two 18-hole courses.

Paradise Golf & Arcade, 3300 North Croatan Highway, Kill Devil Hills. This park features not only golf but also go-karts, bumper-cars, and an arcade.

Galaxy Golf, 2914 South Virginia Dare Trail, Nags Head. A 36-hole course with space-themed obstacles.

Destination Fun, 1217 South Croatan Highway, Kill Devil Hills. This attraction is much more than a miniature golf course. For one thing, the golf is inside. In the dark. With black lights. This 9-hole glow-in-the-dark course features aliens, flying saucers, and asteroids. There's also laser-tag and a 60-game arcade.

Mutiny Bay Adventure Golf, 6704 South Croatan Highway., Nags Head. This is a pirate-themed 18-hole course where you may take cannon fire as you play through. There's also an arcade.

Jurassic Putt, 6926 South Croatan Highway, Nags Head. As you might imagine, this is a dinosaur-themed park featuring two courses.

Playgrounds

David Paul Pruitt Jr. Playground - Playground equipment for both younger and older children, including swing sets, a merry-go-round, slide, and jungle gyms. There's also picnic tables and a multi-use path for biking and jogging.

Location: 5160 The Woods Rd, Kitty Hawk

Hayman Street Park - Enjoy a wide-open space where you can play catch or kick around a soccer ball. Also includes swing sets, a jungle gym, and slides. Or go old school and climb a tree!

Location: West Hayman Street (off Beach Road MP5.5), Kill Devil Hills

Meekins Field - Playground equipment, tennis courts, and a baseball field make this park a great place to get in a good workout or run off some energy.

Location: Beach Road MP 7, Kill Devil Hills

Dowdy Park - Dowdy Park is 5 acres of green space, playground equipment, places to sit, and even checkerboard tables. There are basketball courts, a nature trail, and restrooms. This is a great place to kill some time while waiting to get into your vacation rental. Check their event schedule for summer concerts and other activities.

Location: Corner of South Croatan Highway (Bypass) and Bonnett Street, Nags Head

Insider Tip: On Thursdays during the summer, you can pick up some locally grown fresh vegetables at the farmer's market.

Whalebone Park - This nautical-themed playground across from Jennette's Pier also has shaded picnic tables, plus bocce and volleyball courts.

Location: 7300 South Virginia Dare Trail (Beach Road MP 16.5), Nags Head, (252) 441-5508

Water Life

Jennette's Pier - Jennette's Pier features educational programs, live animal exhibits, and demonstrations of alternative energy sources. Learn basic fishing skills, with all bait and equipment provided, or go on a ghost crab hunt.

Location: Beach Road MP 16

North Carolina Aquarium on Roanoke Island - In addition to enjoying and up-close-and-personal view of exotic sea life, the aquarium offers daily programs that include free educational films, shipwreck stories, and even a chance to participate in feeding the sharks and stingrays.

Location: 374 Airport Road, Manteo, (252) 475-2300

Water Park

H2OBX Waterpark - You'll find pirates, buried treasure, windswept dunes, and wild horses, all the things that make the Outer Banks famous come alive at this waterpark! Get your thrills on more than 30 rides, slides, and attractions, or kick back and enjoy some of their resort amenities — toss a tube in a lazy river or relax under a shaded cabana. With two wave pools and lots of interactive adventures for the little ones, there's something for everyone. Plan a stop on your way to the Outer Banks or plan a day of your vacation to enjoy sliding, splashing, and chilling!

Location: 8526 Caratoke Highway, Powells Point, (252) 491-3000

Chapter 9 - Rainy Day Activities

In a perfect world, every day would be a great beach day. But it has to rain sometime. Hopefully it won't be for the entire week that you're in the OBX, but truthfully, that's happened to us more than once. Hurricane season runs from June 1st to November 1st, and when you're making your reservations months in advance, there's no way to predict whether a storm will spin up the east coast right smack in the middle of your vacation. Even if it doesn't make a direct hit on the Outer Banks, a hurricane or nor'easter can spell weather disaster for your stay.

Insider Tip: If a hurricane is threatening just before or during your stay, have a plan. Stay on top of local news and weather forecasts, and if you're told to evacuate, *evacuate*. So-called "hurricane parties" are both legendary and deadly. In addition, if your power goes out or the roads flood, it could be not just uncomfortable but dangerous. This will be a time to exercise your best judgement. We once rented a house for the 4th of July, which fell on a Friday. By Thursday, we had decided we needed to leave. As it turned out, we could have stayed, and it would have been fine, but we had no way to know that. I can't stress it enough: *Do not take chances with a hurricane. It's just not worth the risk.*

Hopefully, you will not have to contend with a hurricane or a storm system that decides to park itself over the Outer Banks, but there's a good chance you will encounter a rainy day at some point during your stay. This is another scenario where it's a good idea to have a plan. So, in this chapter, I'll give you some ideas for what you can do to keep everyone occupied while you wait for the sun to return.

Insider Tip: The most accurate weather forecasts are going to be found on the network affiliate TV stations that serve the Outer Banks: WAVY - Channel 10 (NBC), WTKR - Channel 3 (CBS), and WVEC - Channel 13 (ABC). Other networks like The Weather Channel are going to give you a bigger picture but won't be as precise and localized as the channels listed above. The same is true for internet sources. The most reliable internet weather forecast is the NOAA site. Most radio stations will provide fairly accurate forecasts, but they usually get their information from the local TV stations.

Library

Kill Devil Hills Library - Unless you have a Dare County library card, you can't check out books or other materials, but they have daily story times for kids, as well as magazines, computers, and wi-fi access. It's also a great place to browse Outer Banks historical information and maps.

Location: 400 Mustian Street, Kill Devil Hills, (252) 441-4331

Shopping

A rainy day is the perfect time to see what the Outer Banks' many unique stores have to offer. I have a complete list of one-of-a-kind stores in Chapter 12.

One store chain that is not particularly unique is Wings. As you drive down the bypass (Rt. 58), you will undoubtedly notice several large stores with bright yellow facades, all sporting the same name: Wings. Just about every town from Corolla to Hatteras has a Wings store. Some towns have more than one. Wings has everything you could possibly need for your stay on the Outer Banks. Need beach equipment? You can find chairs, umbrellas, and towels. Looking for a souvenir tee-shirt or sweatshirt? Wings has you covered, in sizes ranging from infants to 5XL. If you could use a pair of water shoes or flip-flops, Wings has every color imaginable. There's a whole section devoted to Outer Banks coffee cups, beer glasses, water bottles, and shot glasses, plus a selection of souvenir items you would likely find in any beach souvenir shop up and down the east coast — only the names are changed. You can find sunscreen, sunglasses, and wide-brimmed hats, along with home decor, keychains, and wind chimes.

Insider Tip: Every Wings is basically the same. You won't find anything significantly different about the Wings in Kitty Hawk versus the Wings in Hatteras. If you visit the Outer Banks after Labor Day, you will find that every Wings store has a 50% off sale going on. Every item in every store is 50% off. No fine print. It's not buy one, get one at 50% off. Walk in any store after Labor Day, look at the price on the item, and know it will ring up at half of whatever the price tag says. You can get some terrific bargains on everything they sell.

Take in a movie

R/C Kill Devil Hills Movies 10 - Stadium seating, wall-to-wall curved screens, 3-D films, game room, and daily matinees.

Location: 1803 North Croatan Highway, Kill Devil Hills, (252) 441-5630

Insider Tip: A lot of other vacationers will have the same idea about heading to a movie when the weather is bad. Buy your tickets ahead of time online and be prepared to circle the parking lot a few times before you find a spot.

Curl up with a good book

It's likely you will find a take-one/leave-one library at your OBX rental house, but it never hurts to plan ahead and bring along a good book or two. If you want to stick with your Outer Banks theme and immerse yourself in a book set in the OBX, check out some of these titles:

Fiction

- Return to the Outer Banks House
- Home Sweet Outer Banks Home? (Home To The Outer Banks Book 1)
- Home Sweet Outer Banks Home: The Story Continues
- Boss of the Outer Banks
- Buffalo City Moonshine Murders: An Outer Banks Mystery
- Family Business: An Outer Banks Crime Mystery
- Uncharted Deception on the Outer Banks
- The Ghost Fixer (An OBX Haunting)

Nonfiction

- Hidden History of the Outer Banks
- Did You See That? On The Outer Banks: A GPS Guide to the Out of the Ordinary Attractions on the North Carolina Coast
- Outer Banks
- Vintage Outer Banks: Shifting Sands & Bygone Beaches

- Lost Restaurants of the Outer Banks and Their Recipes (American Palate)
- North Carolina Lighthouses: The Stories Behind the Beacons from Cape Fear to Currituck Beach
- Graveyard of the Atlantic: Shipwrecks of the North Carolina Coast
- U-Boats off the Outer Banks: Shadows in the Moonlight (Military)

Chapter 10 - But Wait! There's More!

Believe or not, I haven't covered everything you can do in the Outer Banks. Here are some other activities to check out.

Art Galleries

Glen Eure's Ghost Fleet Gallery - Here you'll find art of all kinds, from oil canvases and watercolors to woodcuts and etchings. Glen Eure was a local artist who designed the building that houses the museum and also helped design the Monument to a Century of Flight in Kitty Hawk.

Location: 210 East Driftwood Street (Gallery Row), Nags Head, (252) 441-6584

Muse Originals - Housed in a historic former firehouse, the mission of this gallery is to help local artists sell their work. With more than 75 artisans, the gallery features an eclectic mix of art, including hand-blown glass, jewelry, and artsy apparel.

Location: 4622 North Virginia Dare Trail (Beach Road MP 2.5), Kitty Hawk, (252) 564-2038

Seaside Art Gallery - Locally owned and operated since 1961, this is one of the largest private galleries in the southeast. Stop by to enjoy one of their monthly art shows or browse for a work of art to take home with you.

Location: 2716 South Virginia Dare Trail (Beach Road), Nags Head, (252) 441-5418

Seagreen Gallery - This is one of my personal favorites. This gallery specializes in repurposing everything from license plates to windows and anything else you can think of, turning it into beautiful works of art. Out back is a delightful garden with more art, farm antiques, driftwood, and more, plus goldfish ponds, rabbits, and birds.

Location: 2404 South Virginia Dare Trail (Beach Road), Nags Head, (252) 715-2426

Golf

Sea Scape Golf Links - This course makes use of the dunes and maritime forest, with dramatic elevation and ocean views.

Location: 300 Eckner Street, Kitty Hawk, (252) 261-2158

Nags Head Golf Links - Try out this Scottish links style championship golf course that overlooks the ocean.

Location: 5615 South Seachase Drive, Nags Head

Horseback Riding

A horseback ride on the beach is something you and your family will never forget. Think of the photo opportunities! Enjoy a quiet ride while you listen to the sound of the waves.

Outer Banks Horseback Ride, Bodie Island Lighthouse Road. & NC-12, Nags Head, (252) 573-8044

Jetpak Lessons

For something *really* different, try a jetpak lesson, also known as flyboarding. You strap one of these on and high-pressure water jets propel you up to 30 feet in the air. This is another activity that will have your adrenaline pumping!

Kitty Hawk Kites - Take a jetpak or flyboard lesson, taking off from a stable pontoon boat called a launchpad.

Location: 307 Queen Elizabeth Avenue, Manteo, (252) 473-2357

Karaoke

Jolly Roger - Bring out your inner *American Idol* and head to the Jolly Roger for nightly karaoke, Tuesday through Saturday at 10:00 p.m. For some visitors, this is on their "must do" list. Trust me, you'll have a blast!

Location: 1836 North Virginia Dare Trail, Kill Devil Hills, (252) 441-6530

YMCA

The Outer Banks YMCA in Nags Head maintains a guest policy for vacationers between May 1st and September 30th. If you happen to live in South Hampton Roads (Virginia) and you are a member of the YMCA, you have full access to the Outer Banks facility. If you're a member from another area, you can buy a one-day guest pass for $5. For non-members, it costs $10. You can also purchase a flex pass that gives you access for 10 days. For an individual, the cost is $75. For a family, which is defined as a parent (or parents) and dependents under the age of 23, the cost is $95. Some hotels and vacation rental homes have an arrangement with the YMCA that will allow you to use the facility at no additional charge. Be sure to ask when you make your reservation. Check the OBX YMCA's guest policy webpage for additional information.

Location: 3000 South Croatan Highway (Bypass), Nags Head, (252) 449-8897

Chapter 11 - Restaurants

Needless to say, most people on vacation would prefer not to spend a lot of time in the kitchen. You probably won't want to go out for every meal, but you may want to have breakfast out at least once and go out for dinner a couple of times. In this chapter, I'll list several restaurants in Kitty Hawk, Kill Devil Hills, and Nags Head, as well as restaurants with multiple locations. Most of these places are well established and should be around for a while, but keep in mind that local businesses come and go. Please also be mindful that, between Memorial Day and Labor Day, restaurants can get very crowded. Particularly if you have a large group, the wait is sometimes lengthy.

I've also included a list of restaurants that deliver. You can find it in this chapter, following the listing of restaurants with multiple locations, and also in Chapter 3 under "What to bring."

If you're looking for a place where you can get a good cup of fresh ground coffee, maybe pick up a croissant or pastry, and enjoy a refreshing freshly squeezed juice drink, check the end of this chapter for a list of coffee shops.

Kitty Hawk Restaurants

Cosmos Pizza – Technically, Cosmos is in Southern Shores, but it's located just after you cross the Wright Memorial Bridge, in the Food Lion shopping center. Their New York-style pizza is the best! They also have salads, pasta, and subs. If you have a craving for a really good pizza, try Cosmos. (Just take note that they close between 3:00 p.m. and 5:00 p.m.)

Location: 5591 North Croatan Highway, Southern Shores, (252) 261-8388

High Cotton Barbecue - Eastern North Carolina barbecue is the best, and nobody does it better than High Cotton. Their barbecue is slow roasted to perfection over hickory coals. Or try their southern fried chicken and hushpuppies. Wash it down with sweet tea and be sure to save room for their chess pie.

Location: 5230 North Virginia Dare Trail (Beach Road MP 2), Kitty Hawk, (252) 255-2275

Rundown Cafe - Named after a Jamaican seafood and coconut soup, Rundown Cafe offers a blend of Pacific rim and Caribbean cuisine. Try the namesake soup, a noodle bowl, or one of their delicious seafood dishes. Pull up a stool at the Tsunami bar for an exotic drink or dine alfresco while enjoying an amazing view of the ocean.

Location: 5218 N Virginia Dare Trail, (Beach Road MP 2), Kitty Hawk, (252) 255-0026

Argyle's - Featuring free-range wild game, grass-fed beef, and fresh local seafood, Argyle's has been operating in Kitty Hawk for over 25 years. Now serving breakfast, as well, you'll find menu selections ranging from eggs Benedict Oscar to tender crepes.

Location: 4716 North Croatan Highway (Bypass MP 2.5), Kitty Hawk, (252) 261-7325

Ocean Boulevard Bistro & Martini Bar - One of my personal favorites, you can sit on the deck of this lovely little restaurant and enjoy both the view and the sound from the ocean. Offering an eclectic seasonal menu, they've been featured in both *Southern Living* and *The Washington Post*. They frequently have live music on the ocean-side patio in the summer.

Location: 4700 North Virginia Dare Trail (Beach Road MP 2.5), Kitty Hawk, (252) 261-2546

Art's Place - Art's is one of the rare OBX restaurants open year-round. Try them for breakfast or for one of their famous burgers made from fresh-ground beef and served with hand-cut fries. My personal recommendation is the Mushroom Swiss burger served on marble rye. They have a full-service bar and daily happy hour specials. Check out the roof-top deck for breathtaking ocean views. Stop in on Monday evening for live jazz or warm up your vocals and join them for karaoke on Wednesdays.

Location: 4624 N. Virginia Dare Trail (Beach Road MP 2.5), Kitty Hawk, (252) 261-3233

Sandtrap Tavern - Local homegrown specialties prepared from scratch. Try their $5 breakfast or stop in for lunch or dinner and enjoy a slow-cooked North Carolina barbecue sandwich or crab cake sandwich. 20-cent shrimp and 75-cent wings at Happy Hour from 3:00 to 6:00! And you can catch your favorite team on one of their 7 big-screen TVs.

Location: 300 West Eckner Street, Kitty Hawk, (252) 261-2243

Bad Bean Baja Grill - Fresh and creative Mexican cuisine, daily specials, and craft beers.

Location: 4146 North Croatan Highway (Bypass MP 3.5), Kitty Hawk, (252) 261-1300

Jimmy's Seafood Buffet - A seafood buffet with a Caribbean twist, you'll find selections ranging from Alaskan snow crab legs to glazed Asian salmon, Bang Bang shrimp, and crab-stuffed mushrooms. Check their website for family-friendly activities and specials.

Location: 4117 North Carolina Highway (Bypass MP 3.5), Kitty Hawk, (252) 261-4973

Shipwrecks Taphouse & Grill - Recently opened and known as The Wreck, this is a great place to hang out while you're waiting to get into your rental. Play some cornhole, snack on smoked rockfish crab dip, or have a burger and a brew. Dine on the deck and enjoy live music (in season) or catch your favorite team on one of their 17 flat-screen TVs.

Location: 4020 North Croatan Highway. Kitty Hawk, (252) 221-5205

Sanya Sushi Bar - Complete sushi bar with all your favorites. You'll also find hibachi shrimp, chicken, beef, lobster, and hibachi vegetables. In the mood for Chinese? Try the sweet & sour chicken, chicken teriyaki, or General Tso's chicken.

Location: 3919 North Croatan Highway (Bypass MP 4), Kitty Hawk, (252) 261-1946

Black Pelican Oceanfront Cafe - Located in a 19th century building once used as a lifesaving station, you'll find lots of character and rustic charm at this restaurant. They offer wood-fired pizza, fresh seafood, and vegetarian dishes. Their daily specials are listed on the home page of their website. The Black Pelican was featured in a 2007 episode of Guy Fieri's *Diners, Drive-Ins, and Dives*. Of even greater significance — my husband and I celebrated our 28th wedding anniversary there.

Location: 3848 Virginia Dare Trail North (Beach Road MP 4), Kitty Hawk, (252) 261-3171

Longboards Island Grill - Casual dining for lunch and dinner, with traditional American bar food selections and dinner entrees, plus handmade pizza. Stop in for a late-night snack and choose from the full menu. Two happy hours daily, from 3:00 to 6:00 p.m. and 11:00 p.m. to 1:00 a.m. Live entertainment, pool tables, karaoke, and a large bar.

Location: 3833 North Croatan Highway (Bypass MP 4, Kitty Hawk, (252) 261-7377

Stack-Em High - As you might guess, Stack-Em High serves up pancakes. But they serve up a lot more than that. Whether you're in the mood for bacon and eggs, waffles with strawberries, or shrimp and grits, you can get it here.

Location: 3801 North Croatan Highway (Bypass MP4), Kitty Hawk, (252) 261-8221

Barefoot Bernie's Tropical Grill & Bar - A wonderful blend of Asian, Mediterranean, and Caribbean cuisine, including an extensive kid's menu, this family atmosphere welcomes everyone, and you can cheer on your favorite sports team on one of their 20 flat screen TVs. From comfort food like New England clam chowder and deviled eggs to tacos and gourmet pizza, along with 16 rotating beers on tap, there's truly something for everyone at Barefoot Bernie's.

Location: 3730 North Croatan Highway (Bypass MP 4.5), Kitty Hawk, (252) 261-1008

Trio Restaurant & Market - Feed your passion at Trio, with wine, beer, cheese, and what they refer to as "casually inventive" food. With an extensive wine list and 24 rotating beer taps, you'll find the perfect beverage to go with their cheese and antipasti plates, salads, paninis, or a cast-iron seared New York strip.

Location: 3708 North Croatan Highway (Bypass MP 4.5), Kitty Hawk, (252) 261-0277

Kill Devil Hills Restaurants

Two Roads Tavern - 20 TVs make this a great place to catch the game. They offer wings, burgers, sandwiches, seafood, and vegan selections, plus craft beer and a full bar. Try their crab cake sandwich, bacon gravy fries, or quinoa burger.

Location: 3105 North Croatan Highway (Bypass MP 5.5), Kill Devil Hills, (252) 255-1980

Chili Peppers - With its global menu and weekly tapas selections, you're sure to find a dish to satisfy your cravings, many prepared with fresh vegetables from the restaurant's own garden. Go out back to visit the garden, eat your meal at a picnic table, or play cornhole. Stop by on Sunday for brunch or drop in for late night munchies.

Location: 3001 North Croatan Highway (Bypass MP 5.5), Kill Devil Hills, (252) 441-8081

Awful Arthur's Oyster Bar - This place is one of our favorites. I don't claim to be a foodie, but I do know what I like, and I think their steamed shrimp is the best on the beach. But there's no need to just take my word for it. Awful Arthur's was recognized by *Esquire* for its shrimp, and *Coastal Living* called it one of America's greatest oyster bars. If you're serious about your seafood, this is the place for you. They offer oysters by the half-pound up to a peck, steamed shrimp, clams by the dozen or half-dozen, and snow crab legs. When they're in season, you can also find soft shell crabs. If yours is a party of two or three, I recommend sitting at the copper-topped bar. You can watch the shrimp and oysters come right out of the steamer. Or head upstairs for a fabulous view of the ocean.

Location: 2106 N Virginia Dare Trail (Beach Road MP 6), Kill Devil Hills, (252) 441-5955

Jolly Roger Restaurant & Bar - The Jolly Roger is a favorite with both locals and vacationers, and is one of our go-to places for breakfast. Formerly a gas station and grocery store, the building was converted to an Italian restaurant in 1972 and has a delightfully tacky and random pirate theme. Everything is made from scratch, including their bread. Be sure to pick up a loaf or two to take home with you before you leave. No matter what you're craving — a hearty breakfast, steak, seafood, pasta, or a late-night snack — the Jolly Roger is the place to go.

Location: 1836 N. Virginia Dare Trail (Beach Road MP 6.75), Kill Devil Hills, (252) 441-6530

Sandbars Raw Bar & Grill - Sandbars offers a raw bar, tacos, wings, and sliders. You can choose where your oysters come from: Striker Bay, Bodie Island, Rochambeau or the James River. Enjoy wine or a craft beer with your meal. Their late-night menu offers a good selection till 1:00 a.m. Check their website for daily specials.

Location: 1716 North Croatan Highway (Bypass MP 7), Kill Devil Hills, (252) 715-2882

Goombays Grille & Raw Bar - A casual island-style atmosphere for tropical drinks and fresh seafood. Offering more than 50 craft beers, there's always a good time to be had at Goombays.

Location: 1608 North Virginia Dare Trail (Beach Road MP 7), Kill Devil Hills, (252) 441-6001

Outer Banks Brewing Station - The Outer Banks Brewing Station is the first wind-powered brewery in the United States. They are easy to find! Just look for the windmill! It's truly one of the most unique places you will find on the Outer Banks. They offer a variety of unique appetizers and entrees ranging from shrimp and grits to pan-seared scallops. They're also known for live entertainment. Brewery tours every Wednesday!

Location: 600 South Croatan Highway (Bypass MP 8.5), Kill Devil Hills, (252) 449-2739

Secret Island Tavern - If you've been to the Outer Banks before, you may remember this restaurant as the Port O'Call. Open for dinner, it's known mainly for its nightlife. DJs, karaoke, and pool tournaments mean there's something going on every night. Check their website for a complete schedule.

Location: 504 South Virginia Dare Trail (Beach Road MP 8.5), Kill Devil Hills (252) 441-7484

Bonzer Shack - A laid-back restaurant serving old school beach comfort food like bacon-wrapped shrimp, fresh tuna, and burgers. Consult their website for daily specials.

Location: 1200 South Virginia Dare Trail (Beach Road MP 9), Kill Devil Hills, (252) 480-1010

Dare Devil's Pizzeria - Family-owned, featuring pizza, stromboli, salads, and sandwiches, plus a full bar. Eat in or carry-out.

Location: 1112 S Virginia Dare Trail (Beach Road MP 9), Kill Devil Hills, (252) 441-6330

JK's Restaurant - Even seafood lovers get a craving for a steak every once in a while, and JK's is the place to go. Midwest beef is hand cut in-house. They also offer ribs and fresh local seafood. Elegant, yet comfortable and not pretentious.

Location: 1106 South Croatan Highway (Bypass MP 9), Kill Devil Hills, (252) 441-9555

Bob's Grill - Bob's Grill is perhaps most famous for their tagline: *Eat and Get the Hell Out!* For many people, Bob's is their go-to choose for breakfast. Serving both breakfast and lunch choices all day, their friendly staff actually will never make you feel rushed. Choose a three-egg omelet, a stack of their huge pancakes, or if you prefer, have a BLT or a burger. Enjoy a bloody Mary, mimosa, or screwdriver with your omelet and pancakes or have a cold beer to wash down your burger.

Location: 1219 South Croatan Highway (Bypass MP 9), Kill Devil Hills, (252) 441-0707.

Millers Seafood & Steakhouse - Family-owned, serving breakfast and dinner, sushi and local beers. The owners love to make the rounds and check on diners to ensure they have everything they need. They are happy to accommodate large groups.

Location: 1520 South Virginia Dare Trail (Beach Road MP 9.5), (252) 441-7674

Kill Devil Grill - With unique menu items such as cheesesteak egg rolls and beer can shrimp, it's no wonder this place is so popular. Their "Big Plates" will satisfy even the heartiest appetite, or you can choose a Big Kahuna Burger (with a nod to *Pulp Fiction*). Good wine list, yummy dessert menu — it's worth the wait.

Location: 2008 South Virginia Dare Trail (Beach Road MP 9.75), Kill Devil Hills, (252) 449-8181

Mama Kwan's Tiki Bar & Grill - This award-winning restaurant offers seafood, wings, and tacos, all with an Asian twist. You'll find a long list of shooters and frozen drinks, plus beer and wine. Fun and relaxed, it's one of our go-to places.

Location: 1701 South Croatan Highway (Bypass), Kill Devil Hills, (252) 441-7889

Country Deli - With a wide variety of sandwiches, salads, and grilled cheese, Country Deli is the perfect lunch choice. They also offer an all-day breakfast menu. Their hefty portions, party trays, and three-foot party subs are sure to satisfy even the heartiest appetite. Plus, they deliver! If you're located between MP 5.5 and MP 17, all you have to do is call.

Location: 1900 South Croatan Highway (Bypass MP 9.75), Kill Devil Hills, (252) 441-5684

Nags Head Restaurants

Red Drum Grille & Taphouse - Locally owned and named for a favorite Outer Banks catch, the Red Drum offers something for everyone. From fresh local seafood to steaks, ribs, and chicken, the Red Drum is a casual and relaxed family-friendly restaurant.

Location: 2412 South Virginia Dare Trail (Beach Road MP 10), Nags Head, (252) 480-1095

New York Pizza Pub Italian Grill - Featuring hand-tossed New York style pizza. Buy a whole pie or by the slice. You can also indulge your craving for Italian dishes such as lasagna and chicken parm. Everything is made from scratch. With 28 TVs, it's also a great place to cheer on your favorite sports teams, or catch some live music. They offer a fully stocked bar and over 30 beer selections. They even deliver!

Location: 2217 S. Croatan Highway (Bypass MP 10), Nags Head, (252) 441-2660

Viva Mexican Grill - This build-your-own taco bar is quick, casual, and wallet-friendly. Choose a burrito, quesadilla, or nachos, and wash it down with an ice-cold "cerveza."

Location: 2424 South Croatan Highway (Bypass MP 10.5), Nags Head, (252) 441-1601

Tortuga's Lie - Featured on Guy Fieri's *Diners, Drive-Ins, and Dives*, Tortuga's Lie serves up everything from Hatteras-style chowder to steamed clams and Jamaican jerk chicken.

Location: 3014 South Virginia Dare Trail (Beach Road MP 11), Nags Head, (252) 441-RAWW

Lucky 12 Tavern - The Lucky 12 is a favorite among both locals and tourists. Their fun, affordable dining includes fresh local seafood, New York style pizza, wings, and my favorite, boardwalk fries. (Don't forget the vinegar!) Serving pizza until 2:00 a.m., it's the perfect spot for a late-night bite. They offer 90 different beers, 20 of them on tap, including local craft beers. In the mood for wine or a martini? They've got you covered. With 20 big-screen TVs, including 3 on the patio, you can watch your favorite team while you dine.

Location: 3308 South Virginia Dare Trail (Beach Road MP 11.5), Nags Head, (252) 255-5825

Mulligan's Grille - Mulligan's is famous for authentic coastal dining, including an oyster bar, and the best burger on the beach. Their shrimp and oysters are locally harvested in the Pamlico Sound, and they recycle everything, from their vegetable oil to their oyster shells. With three fully stocked bars, including their award-winning covered Tiki Deck, choose one of their famous crush drinks, a custom martini, or an ice-cold beer. They are one of the few Outer Banks restaurants open 365 days a year. Check their website for daily specials.

Location: 4005 South Croatan Highway (Bypass MP 13), Nags Head, (252) 480-2000

Blue Moon Beach Grill - Quirky and fun-filled, this is a small restaurant that offers Southern comfort food with flair. Try the buffalo shrimp or the Caribbean pulled pork sandwich. They offer seafood dishes from fish tacos to seaside bucatini. There's a full bar with local craft beers and a wine list.

Location: 4104 South Virginia Dare Trail (Beach Road MP 13), Nags Head, (252) 261-2583

Grits Grill - This little place is one of our favorites. Open for breakfast and lunch, enjoy southern grits, homemade biscuits, omelets, burgers, sandwiches, and more. We always try to get to the Grits Grill whenever we're in the Outer Banks.

Location: 5000 South Croatan Highway (Bypass MP14), (252) 449-2888

Pamlico Jack's - Enjoy light fare and tapas, steamer plates and filet mignon. If you're looking for the perfect location to dine and watch the sunset, look no further. A romantic sunset dinner here provided a beautiful setting for my son's proposal to his beautiful bride. The restaurant posts sunset times daily on their road sign.

Location: 6708 South Croatan Highway (Bypass MP 16), Nags Head, (252) 441-2637

(Note: As of publication date, Pamlico Jack's remains open for business. However, my understanding is that the property has been sold to the Town of Nags Head for the purpose of expanding their festival grounds, so please check the status of the restaurant before making your plans.)

The Dunes - Stop in for breakfast, dinner, or enjoy cocktails at the bar. This family-owned restaurant offers both southern hospitality and contemporary dining. Check their website for their all-you-can-eat crab legs!

Location: 7013 South Croatan Highway (Bypass MP 16), Nags Head

Sam & Omie's - One of the oldest restaurants on the Outer Banks and one of the most popular for breakfast. Beachy and relaxed, pop in for a burger at lunch or prime rib for dinner. Sam & Omie's has a rich history and will definitely become one of your favorites.

Location: 7228 South Virginia Dare Trail (Beach Road MP 16.5), Nags Head, (252) 441-7366

Basnight's Lone Cedar Cafe - Specializing in fresh and local Outer Banks Seafood, enjoy waterfront dining at Basnight's. Seafood is caught daily by local fisherman and served up with farm-to-table vegetables and even some ingredients grown in their on-site chemical-free garden. While you dine, you can enjoy a breathtaking view of the sunset. Live music on Friday, Saturday, Sunday nights.

Location: 7623 S. Virginia Dare Trail (Manteo Causeway), Nags Head, (252) 441-5405

Freshfit Cafe - Even when we're on vacation, many of us want to stay (at least somewhat) health conscious. This is a health-oriented cafe and juice bar serving up balanced breakfast and lunch choices, as well as organic coffee, espresso, a juice bar, and smoothies. They use local seafood, fresh seasonal fruits and veggies, and clean protein choices. They also have a kid's menu, and best of all, they're right on the water.

Location: 7531 S Virginia Dare Trail (Manteo Causeway), Nags Head, (252) 715-6444.

Fish Heads Bar & Grill - For dining with a view of the water, you won't get any closer than this. Located on the Outer Banks Pier, they feature 33 craft brews on tap, daily happy hour specials, including steamed shrimp, plus salads and sandwiches. Check the music calendar on their website for a schedule of live music.

Location: 8901 South Old Oregon Inlet Road (Beach Road), Nags Head, (252) 441-5740.

Sugar Creek Seafood Restaurant - In addition to it being a full-service seafood restaurant, there is also a seafood market on premises. Enjoy a beautiful view of the water while dining on fresh local seafood. Locally owned, their menu offers traditional southern cuisine such as fried green tomatoes, seafood entrees, salads, and sandwiches.

Location: 7340 S Virginia Dare Trail (Manteo Causeway), Nags Head, (252) 441-4963

Restaurants with Multiple Locations

La Fogata Mexican Restaurant - In the mood for some authentic Mexican food? This is your place. Dine-in or carryout, La Fogata (which translates as "the fire") is a family-owned casual dining experience. They're able to accommodate large parties and accept reservations (although they are not required). Fresh food made daily and a full bar.

Locations:

- 3924 North Croatan Highway (Bypass), Kitty Hawk, (252) 255-0934
- 4933 North Croatan Highway (Bypass), Nags Head, (252) 441-4179
- 41934 NC-12, Avon, (252) 986-1118

Pizzazz Pizza - Whether it's your first night of vacation and you're looking for a quick and easy meal or perhaps a rainy evening settling in to watch a movie, sometimes a good pizza is just what you need. Pizzazz is a locally owned family restaurant and uses fresh ingredients to make their pizza from scratch every day. Reach all four locations at (252) 261-1111.

Locations:

- 2512 South Croatan Highway (Bypass), Nags Head, (252) 261-1111
- 109 Forbes Loop, Grandy, (252) 453-2800
- 603 Currituck Clubhouse Drive, Corolla, (252) 453-8858
- 1187 Duck Road, Duck, (252) 261-8822

Duck Donuts - Many people say that no trip to the Outer Banks is complete without a Duck Donut. Originating in Duck, North Carolina, they have expanded into a franchise organization with dozens of locations across the country.

Outer Banks Locations:

- 5230 North Virginia Dare Trail (Beach Road), Kitty Hawk, (252) 261-3312

- 710 South Croatan Highway (Bypass), Kill Devil Hills, (252) 480-3320

- 5000 South Croatan Highway (Bypass), Nags Head, (252) 255-5730

- 1190 Duck Road, Duck, (252) 480-3304

- 41934 NC-12, Avon, (252) 995-9950

Restaurants that deliver

At time of publication, neither GrubHub nor DoorDash was serving the Outer Banks. However, there are several restaurants that will deliver to your vacation rental, and you're not limited to just pizza. You can even get beer and wine delivered!

Max's Italian Restaurant - Salads, pizza, stromboli, calzones, pasta, subs, paninis, and desserts.

Call: 252-261-3113

Country Deli - If you love a good sandwich, you'll love the Country Deli. Try one of their "Famous Pounders," a Triple-Decker, one of a dozen other specialty sandwiches or a classic deli sandwich. They also have vegetarian choices, salads, and grilled cheese.

Call: (252) 441-5684

Slice Pizzeria - Not just pizza. They also have salads, subs, calzones, stromboli, pasta, and desserts.

Call: (252) 449-8888

Colington Pizza - If you're staying in Colington, they will be happy to deliver to you. Build your own pizza or stromboli, or order a sub, sandwich, or salad.

Call: (252) 441-3339

Sal's New York Pizza - Sandwiches, salads, hot and cold subs, pasta, and of course, pizza.

Call: (252) 715-3145

Nags Head Pizza Company - Specialty pizzas and build-your-own salads.

Call: (252) 715-3455

Pizzazz Pizza - Delivering pizza, of course, and also wings, salads, and subs.

Call: (252) 261-1111

South Beach - Bowls, wraps, sandwiches, cheesesteaks, burgers, salads, and even selections for your furry family member.

Call: (252) 255-1698

Domino's Pizza - If you're a fan of Domino's, you're in luck! (Pretty sure they will even bring it out to the beach for you if you want!)

Call: (252) 441-1525

Pizza Hut - For fans of The Hut, you can have all your favorites delivered.

Call: (252) 441-7101

Papa John's - Can't live without the garlic dipping sauce? PJ's has you covered at the beach.

Call: (252) 261-2389

Coffee Shops

Outer Bean Cafe - Offering a variety of breakfast choices, from eggs to bagels, including vegetarian and vegan choices, as well as organic free-trade coffee, juice, and smoothies.

Location: 3701 North Croatan Highway (Bypass MP 4.5), Kitty Hawk, (252) 261-6000

Front Porch Cafe - A variety of fresh roasted coffee and tea, as well as merchandise.

Locations:

2200 North Croatan Highway (Bypass), Kill Devil Hills, (252) 449-6616

2515 South Croatan Highway (Bypass), Nags Head, (252) 480-6616

300 South Highway 64/264, Manteo, (252) 473-3160

Waverider's Coffee, Deli & Pub - Grab a coffee, latte, espresso, or tea, or try one of a dozen varieties of their smoothies — or build your own. Also offering breakfast sandwiches, deli sandwiches, paninis, salads, and burgers. If you're in the mood for something a bit stronger, go for a beer flight, mimosa flight, or a glass of wine.

Location: 3022 South Croatan Highway (Bypass), Nags Head, (252) 715-1880

Morning View Coffee House - In-house roasting means your coffee will always be fresh roasted. They also offer espresso, tea, and bagels and pastries.

Location: 2707 South Croatan Highway (Bypass), Nags Head, (252) 441-4474

Chapter 12 - Shopping

The Outer Banks has some wonderfully unique stores and shops, and provides many opportunities to shop locally owned businesses. In this chapter, I'll provide a directory of local stores that offer products that are out of the ordinary.

Kitty Hawk

Island Bookstore - An independent bookstore offering books on every subject, from local history to fiction, cooking, crafts, children's books, and more. They also carry a large selection of magazines. You'll find unique gifts — handcrafted leather journals, gift bags and tote bags, and a variety of jigsaw puzzles. Check their website for employee reading recommendations.

Location: 3712 North Croatan Highway (Bypass), Kitty Hawk, (252) 255-5590

Kill Devil Hills

Make It Personal - Pick up a unique personalized gift, anything from baby items to Christmas ornaments to your favorite sports team. They engrave on almost anything, and they also do watch and jewelry repair.

Location: 3105 North Croatan Highway (Bypass MP 5.5), Kill Devil Hills, (252) 255-5222

Chip's Wine & Beer - Chip's is a family-run store that boasts the largest selection of wine and beer on the Outer Banks. Visit their tasting lounge to enjoy a pint of beer, a glass of wine, or samples.

Location: 2200 North Croatan Highway (Bypass MP 6), Kill Devil Hills, (252) 449-8229

Outer Banks Olive Oil Company - Shop for fresh extra virgin olive oil and specialty vinegars. Over 60 varieties available for tasting. You'll also find gourmet foods, cheese, and chocolate.

Location: 2200 North Croatan Highway (Bypass MP 6), Kill Devil Hills, (252) 449-8229

The Bird Store - This store is the opposite of the cookie-cutter souvenir shops you'll find along the bypass. Here you'll find a gallery of antique decoys, locally carved decoys, and original art, as well as antique fishing and hunting gear. Or pick up a nice piece of driftwood to take home. You can tell your friends you found it at the beach! (Because you did!)

Location: 807 South Croatan Highway (Bypass MP 8 ½), Kill Devil Hills, (252) 480-2951

Nags Head Hammocks - Take a piece of Outer Banks living home with you — or have it shipped direct to your home. You'll find hammocks, swings, teak furniture, and accessories.

Location: 1801 South Croatan Highway (Bypass), Kill Devil Hills, (252) 441-6115

American Classics Garage - If you're into vintage cars and decor, you're going to love this place! They carry reproductions of automotive memorabilia, including Dodge, Chevrolet, Ford, and John Deere. If you're looking for decorations for your man cave — or shopping for someone who loves cars — don't miss it!

Location: 1808 South Croatan Highway (Bypass, MP 9.5), Kill Devil Hills, (252) 441-8867

Outer Banks Gourmet Deli & Beach Shop - This store is easy to spot, because it's attached to the Exxon station at the corner of South Virginia Dare Trail and Ocean Bay Boulevard. It's a nice little beach supply shop, plus there's a Boar's Head deli offering made-to-order sandwiches. You'll also find a huge selection of sauces and seasonings for use in your own cooking, and they have wine and beer. You can even order a keg if you're planning a big bash.

Nags Head

Jewelry by Gail - Here you'll find custom-designed fine jewelry in gold, silver, and platinum, with diamonds, pearls, and colored gemstones. Gail is an award-winning designer whose jewelry has been worn by celebrities on the red carpet. She also features other designers in her store, and her pieces are priced to fit into a range of budgets. Stop by and check out her lighthouse jewelry!

Location: 207 East Driftwood Street, Nags Head, (252) 441-5387

Seagreen Gallery - I love this place. They specialize in repurposing everything from license plates to windows and anything else you can think of, turning it into beautiful works of art. Out back is a delightful garden with more art, farm antiques, driftwood, and more, plus goldfish ponds, rabbits, and birds.

Location: 2404 South Virginia Dare Trail (Beach Road), Nags Head, (252) 715-2426

Gulf Stream Gifts - A great place to find gifts and souvenirs that are out of the ordinary. They carry coastal themed fine and fashion jewelry you won't find anywhere else. You'll also find mermaid themed items, Christmas decorations, and even something for your furry family member!

Location: 2512 South Virginia Dare Trail (Beach Road MP 10.5), Nags Head, (252) 441-0433

The Cottage Shop - If you're looking for a unique souvenir or gift idea, definitely check out this place. They have an amazing collection of Outer Banks home accents, furniture, and bedding, plus artwork, jewelry, and lots more.

Location: 5000 South Croatan Highway (Bypass), Nags Head, (252) 441-2522

The Cotton Gin - This is one of my favorite places. Sadly, the location in Jarvisburg, North Carolina, burned to the ground in 2019, but the Nags Head location is still open for business. They carry everything from Tommy Bahama sportswear to Pandora jewelry. I love their coastal living and nautical decor, and you can also find Yankee candles, local wines, and vintage replica signs and memorabilia.

Location: 5151 South Croatan Highway, Nags Head, (252) 449-2387

Pirates and Pixies Toy Store - Family owned and operated since 2010, this toy store has something for everyone — as they put it, "from old school to cutting edge." Toys for newborns to teens.

Location: 7332 South Virginia Dare Trail (Beach Road MP 17), Nags Head, (252) 441-8697

Chapter 13 - Off-Season Activities

Bargain Shopping

As previously mentioned in Chapter 9, one store chain you'll notice in just about every town from Corolla to Hatteras is Wings. They have everything you could possibly need for your stay in the Outer Banks. You can find chairs, umbrellas, and towels, as well as souvenir tee-shirts and sweatshirts. There's a whole section of Outer Banks coffee cups, beer glasses, water bottles, and shot glasses, plus a selection of souvenir items you would likely find in any beach souvenir shop up and down the east coast — only the names are changed. You can find sunscreen, sunglasses, and wide-brimmed hats, along with home decor, keychains, and wind chimes.

If you visit the Outer Banks after Labor Day, you will find that every Wings store has a 50% off sale going on. Every item in every store is 50% off. No fine print. It's not buy one, get one at 50% off. Walk in any store after Labor Day, look at the price on the item, and know it will ring up at half of whatever the price tag says. You can get some terrific bargains on everything they sell. The selection, of course, gets more and more sparse over time, but you can still find some good bargains even well into the fall. Other stores also have clearance sales; just be sure to check the details.

Weather

Even in the off-season, the weather in the Outer Banks is generally mild. High temperatures rarely dip below 50, although lows can sometimes drop into the 30s in January and February. If you want to take advantage of off-season rates but still enjoy relatively warm weather, your best bets are May and September, when highs are typically in the 70s and low 80s, with lows in the 60s.

Outdoor Activities

If you get a nice sunny day without a lot of wind, even the off-season months can be good beach days. You probably won't want to go in the water, but there's no rule that says you can't bundle up if you need to and relax with a novel, play football, cornhole, or other games, or do some beachcombing.

Also consider hiking up Jockey's Ridge, or taking a stroll through Kitty Hawk Woods Reserve or Nags Head Woods Preserve, or visit the Roanoke Marshes Lighthouse. You can also consult my list of Rainy-Day Activities in Chapter 9 for some other ideas of activities for the off-season.

Restaurants

Keep in mind that if you visit the Outer Banks during January or February, most of the restaurants are likely to be closed. There's an Applebee's and an Outback steakhouse in Nags Head that stay open year-round, as well as a few other local establishments, but there's a good chance you're going to be on your own for meals. If you stay in a hotel, as opposed to a vacation home, consider selecting a room with a kitchenette so you can at least cook some of your meals. All the grocery stores in the Outer Banks stay open year-round.

Christmas

The Outer Banks at Christmas can be enchanting. There are plenty of activities, and many restaurants are open through New Year's Day.

Insider Tip: In Kill Devil Hills, head to the west end of Ocean Acres Drive to view a spectacular Christmas wonderland. One family transforms their home into a showcase of colorful lights, vintage trains, snowmen, elves, and much more. Their garage becomes a holiday museum with village scenes and stuffed toys.

Winter Lights at Elizabethan Gardens - The garden paths are transformed into a stunning display of holiday lights for an illuminated winter wonderland. Enjoy traditional holiday decorations and beautiful displays. You'll find festive trees at the Gatehouse and Reception Hall, and an open-air fire on the Great Lawn. There's also a seasonal gift shop and plant sales. Check the website for exact dates and times.

Manteo Christmas Parade - If you're vacationing during the first week of December, be sure to take in the annual Manteo Christmas festivities, always held on the first weekend of December, including a tree lighting followed by a parade the next morning. The parade takes place on Roanoke Island, in the heart of Manteo, and features floats, local high school bands, vintage cars, horses, and of course, the big man himself, Santa Claus! It's a great way to get into the Christmas spirit!

Hangin' With Santa & Kites with Lights - If you visit the Outer Banks during the Thanksgiving weekend, take your kids for free photos with Santa and check out some classic toys in the Kitty Hawk Kites workshop. Don't miss the unique light show on the Saturday after Thanksgiving, featuring 19-to-30-foot kites lit up for the season and the lighting of the Jockey's Ridge State Park solar Christmas tree.

Location: Kitty Hawk Kites, Jockey's Ridge Crossing, Nags Head

Other Off-Season Events

Outer Banks Wedding Weekend & Expo - If you are planning an Outer Banks wedding, this event should be your first stop. Generally held over the first weekend of March, you'll have the opportunity to visit with over 100 wedding vendors and tour some of the most popular OBX wedding venues. It's a chance to meet with caterers, photographers, rental companies, and lots more. Check the website for exact dates and a list of vendors and venues.

Outer Banks Taste of the Beach - Usually held over the last weekend of March, visit the OBX for four days of food, drink, and fun. It's a great opportunity to sample food from different restaurants. Events include wine tastings, cooking classes, brewery tours, tapas crawls, and cookoffs. Check their website for exact dates and list of events.

Flying Pirate Half & First Flight 5K - The Outer Banks Flying Pirate Half-Marathon begins in Kitty Hawk and winds through 13.1 miles of OBX beauty. From the Kitty Hawk Woods Coastal Reserve, along Kitty Hawk Bay and Colington Creek, to the Wright Brothers National Memorial, and finishing at the Nags Head Woods Preserve, you'll be rewarded at the finish line with a Pirate Jamboree featuring live music, food, fun, and beer. There's also a 5K and a Fun Run that skirt around the Wright Brothers monument. Typically held on the third Sunday of April.

Location: 5300 The Woods Road, Kitty Hawk, (252) 255-6273

Hang Gliding Spectacular - This is the world's oldest continually running hang gliding meet. Typically held in May, with four full days of events taking place at various locations. Check the Kitty Hawk Kites website for details.

Outer Banks Seafood Festival - Typically held on the third weekend of October, this festival is a seafood lover's dream. Restaurants from all over the Outer Banks serve up some of their best dishes. Pair your favorites with a local wine or frosty brew, enjoy great live entertainment, and shop at dozens of vendors for unique Outer Banks arts and crafts, educational opportunities, as well as a chance to support local charities.

Location: 6800 South Croatan Highway (Bypass MP 16.5), Nags Head, NC 27959

Chapter 14 - Conserving the Beauty

The main reason people visit the Outer Banks is to drink in the breathtaking beauty and enjoy the natural resources. It's up to all of us, as lovers of the Outer Banks, to help maintain that beauty and preserve it for others.

Leave No Trace

The basic rule of being a responsible beach citizen is to leave nothing behind that indicates you were ever there. This means beach equipment, food containers, toys, and anything else you bring to the beach with you. Items left on the beach can interfere with sea turtle nesting or get washed out to sea, where they could endanger other types of sea-life.

Always bring a trash bag with you. Pick up not only your own trash but any other trash you see.

In addition, limit your use of disposable plastic. This is a good idea in general, since many disposable plastic bottles, straws, and other items end up in our oceans, where they can injure or kill wildlife and sea life. It's especially important when eating or drinking on the beach, since these items can blow away or be accidentally left behind and get washed into the ocean.

Thank You for Not Smoking

If you must smoke, please avoid doing so on the beach. Even though you're outside, the smell can spoil the enjoyment of the salt air for others. And please, whatever you do, **do not use the beach as your ashtray!** There are few things more disgusting than finding the perfect place to plant your beach umbrella for the day, only to discover a pile of cigarette butts in the sand.

Stay Off the Dunes

The dunes are the only protection the islands have from the sea during a storm. Even with the protection of the dunes, it's not unusual for the ocean to cut through them and undermine the foundation of homes and either cover the road with a foot or more of sand or wash out the road completely. The vegetation that grows on the dunes helps to stabilize them and keep them from being washed away.

For this reason, it's critically important that you not walk on the dunes or pick the vegetation. In fact, in most locations, it's illegal to do either. Be sure your kids know how important it is to protect the dunes and help preserve the buildings and roads from the encroaching sea.

Protected Wildlife

One of the things that makes the Outer Banks such a wonderful place to visit is its variety of wildlife, birds, and sea-life. That also means it is vital that all visitors to the area respect the many animals that make the Outer Banks their home. It's also important for visitors to understand that certain species are protected by law.

Wild Horses

The wild horses, mostly inhabiting the four-wheel-drive areas of Corolla, are beautiful and exciting to see, but they must be appreciated from a distance. It is illegal to get within 50 feet of one of these horses. That means, if a horse approaches you, it is your responsibility to move away. Do not pet them or feed them. Doing so can result in a costly fine.

Loggerhead Sea Turtles

This species of turtle has been on the endangered species list since the late 1970s. If you see a sea turtle, it's important to report it to the National Park Service (NPS) by calling (252) 216-6892. This includes turtles you may inadvertently catch while fishing. The only goal for the NPS is to ensure the turtle is safe. You will not be penalized for reporting that you accidentally caught a sea turtle. Nesting season for sea turtle is from July to September. If you come across a sea turtle nest, please keep your distance. Avoid using flashlights or flash photography and keep your pets away from the nest. Do not interfere with either the mother turtle or the excavating babies.

Red Wolf

The red wolf can be seen in the Alligator River National Preserve. It is severely endangered, with only about 55 of them living in the wild.

Chapter 15 - Can't Get Enough?

If you fall in love with the Outer Banks the way I have, you may be thinking "I need to live here!" Or maybe you're seeing dollar signs as you think of the investment possibilities.

> *My dream is to have a house on the beach, even just a little shack somewhere so I can wake up, have coffee, look at dolphins, be quiet and breathe the air.*
> *— Christina Applegate*

At time of publication, you can purchase a condo on the west side of Kill Devil Hills for under $200,000. One of the high-end ocean-front investment properties that can command upwards of $20,000 per week in rent during peak season will run you $2.5 million or more. And needless to say, there's everything in between.

If you're in the market for a permanent or second home, I urge you to spend some time studying the market. As they say with real estate, location is everything, and just because you find a home in the Outer Banks at the right price and the right size doesn't necessarily mean it will be the right location to fit your needs.

For example, that affordable condo? Consider that you may have to compete with other residents for a parking space, lug your groceries up three flights of stairs, put up with noises from upstairs neighbors, and have your time outside on the balcony ruined by a smoker next door.

If you start house hunting online, you may notice some very nice houses at very appealing prices that are located in Kill Devil Hills. There's a good chance these homes will be located in an area called Colington. Much of Colington is beautiful. Some of the homes are inside a gated community and right on the Albemarle Sound. It may be just what you're looking for. It's about five miles from the beach, down a winding two-lane road, and is considered a boater's paradise.

My point is that, like any real estate purchase, it's important to become familiar with the area where you're thinking of buying, for a number of reasons:

- You'll be able to make an educated determination if the home you're considering is fairly priced.
- You'll have a better idea of how long it will take you to get to a grocery store or to get to medical help if you need it.
- You'll be able to identify the flood zone of the property. Needless to say, flooding can be an issue in the Outer Banks, and your insurance costs can vary significantly based on the location of the home.

If, on the other hand, you are thinking about investing in a seasonal rental property, make sure you work with an agent who can provide you with a three-year rental history for the property, as well as a list of expenses you can expect as an owner. Remember that, as an owner, you will be responsible for all the utility costs, in addition to the mortgage and insurance. You should also consider that wear and tear on a seasonal rental home is likely to be beyond that of a year-round rental, a primary residence, or a second home.

Speaking of year-round rentals, this can be an excellent opportunity for building equity in an Outer Banks property. There is a shortage of long-term rentals available in the Outer Banks. Most long-term rentals are only for six months, at most, during the winter months, when demand for seasonal rentals drops off. Investing in a property with the intention of offering a one-year lease is definitely something to look into, depending on your needs and goals.

Chapter 16 - Important Resources

For links to all of the resources listed below, as well as many of the hotel, realty, restaurant, and attraction information — and much more! — visit www.beachloverobx.com.

For Emergencies, Dial 911

Coast Guard - For maritime emergencies, call (757) 398-6231 or use VHF-FM Channel 16 (156.8 MHz), dial 911

Local Government

Town of Kitty Hawk:
- Town Hall (252) 261-3552
- Public Works (252) 261-1367
- Police (252) 261-3895
- Fire Dept. (252) 261-2666

Town of Kill Devil Hills
- Town Hall (252) 449-5300
- Public Works (252) 480-4080
- Police (252) 449-5337
- Fire Dept. (252) 480-4060

Town of Nags Head
- Town Hall (252) 441-5508
- Public Works (252) 441-1122
- Police (252) 441-6386
- Fire Dept. (252) 441-5909

Medical Services

The Outer Banks Hospital (Nags Head)
(252) 449-4500
4800 South Croatan Highway (Bypass)
Nags Head

Outer Banks Hospital Urgent Care (Kitty Hawk)
(252) 449-7474
5112 North Croatan Highway (Bypass)
Kitty Hawk

Outer Banks Hospital Urgent Care (Nags Head)
(252) 261-8040
4923 South Croatan Highway (Bypass)
Nags Head

Animal Rescue

NC Wildlife Helpline
866-318-2401

Wildlife Enforcement Division
800-662-7137

Network for Endangered Sea Turtles (NEST)
(252) 441-8622

Dare County Animal Shelter
(252) 475-5620
After Hours Emergencies: (888) 876-5942

Kill Devil Hills Animal Control Division and Animal Shelter
(252) 480-4047

(If no answer, officer may be on call; leave detailed message.)

Veterinarians

- Outer Banks Veterinary Hospital - (252) 715-1407 (Kitty Hawk)
- Martin's Point Veterinary Hospital (Kitty Hawk)
- Coastal Animal Hospital - (252) 261-2250 (Kitty Hawk, Hatteras)
- Animal Hospital of Nags Head - (252) 441-8611 (Nags Head)
- Gallery Row Animal Hospital - (252) 715-5300 (Nags Head)
- Roanoke Island Animal Clinic - (252) 473-3117 (Manteo)

Vacation Rentals

Airbnb
Beach Realty - (800) 635-1559
Brindley Beach Vacations & Sales - (877) 642-3224
Carolina Designs - (800) 368-3825
Elan Vacations - (800) 458.3830
First Flight Rentals - (866) 595.1893
Joe Lamb, Jr. - (800) 552-6257
Resort Realty - (800) 458-3830
Sea Spray Cottages - (804) 337.7850
Seaside Vacations - (800) 395-2525
Southern Shores Realty - (800) 334-1000
Stan White Realty - (800) 338-3233
Sun Realty - (888) 853-7770
Twiddy - (866) 457-1190
VRBO
Village Realty - (800) 441-8533

Wright Cottage Court - (252) 441-7331

Local TV Affiliates

ABC - WVEC Channel 13
CBS - WTKR Channel 3
FOX - WVBT Channel 43
NBC - WAVY Channel 10

Local News and Newspapers

Island Free Press (252) 888-NEWS
OBX Today (252) 449-6074
The Coastland Times (252) 473-2105
The Outer Banks Voice (857) 205-5161

Local FM Radio Stations

90.9 - WURI - Classical
92.3 - WZPR - Classic Rock
95.3 - WOBR - Rock
98.1 - WOBX - News/Talk
99.1 - WVOD - Adult Album Alternative
100.9 - WFMI - Gospel
104.1 - WCXL - Adult Contemporary

Live Webcams

Avalon Pier, Kill Devil Hills
Sea Ranch Resort, Kill Devil Hills
Jennette's Pier, Nags Head

Attractions

Cape Hatteras Light Station - (252) 473-2111
Jennette's Pier - (252) 255-1501
Jockeys Ridge State Park - (252) 441-7132
Roanoke Island Festival Park - (252) 475-1500
The Elizabethan Gardens - (252) 473-3234
The Lost Colony - (252) 473-6000

Wright Brothers National Memorial - (252) 473-2111

Fishing License

North Carolina Wildlife Resources Commission - (888) 248-6834

For more information, visit *The Beach Lover's Guide* website:

www.beachloverobx.com

Made in United States
North Haven, CT
03 January 2024